THIS
NOBLE
DESTINY

'Abdu'-Bahá with Ali Kuli Khan and Florence Breed Khan
in Washington, D.C.

'Abdu'l-Bahá, the Early Bahá'ís
of Washington, D.C., and the
Struggle for Racial Unity

THIS
NOBLE
DESTINY

Hillary Ioas Chapman & Lex Musta

Kalimat Press
Los Angeles

Library of Congress Control Number: 2024942660

ISBN 978-1-890688-46-2

Photography and Illustrations:
All photographs and art reproduced within are in the public domain or private collection except where noted.

Cover design: Constellation Book Services
Interior design: Steven Scholl

Published by:
Kalimát Press
1600 Sawtelle Boulevard
Suite 310
Los Angeles, CA 90025

www.kalimatpress.com
kalimatpress@gmail.com
Editorial : orders@kalimat.com

Contents

Acknowledgments

The authors would like to thank Mrs. Catherine Chapman-Wong for her many hours of editing and Mr. John Dugas for his generous assistance with and enthusiasm for this work.

Foreword

In 1913, Coralie Cook wrote a brilliant and poignant letter to her "dearly beloved Teacher," 'Abdu'l-Bahá. Her questions and concerns centered on the Baha'i community of Washington, D.C. and its journey toward race unity and justice. The letter reached a crescendo in these words, "The blessed Báb, Bahá'u'lláh, and the Center of the Covenant, have blazed the path for our feet to tread. Dare we turn back?"

Cook was born into slavery, but by the time she penned those lines for her beloved Teacher, she was a leading intellectual, orator, and activist of Washington, D.C. Her rhetorical question—"Dare we turn back?"—signaled the intensity of her commitment to tread the path toward racial equality. For Cook and her fellow travelers in the American Baha'i community, the way forward was shown through the example and guidance of 'Abdu'l-Bahá.

More than a century after Cook took determined steps along her path, racial equality in America still glimmers as a far-off horizon. For some, the distance ahead is forbidding, the goal beyond our capacity. But for others, who have set their sights on that horizon, 'Abdu'l-Bahá remains an unfailing guide. In the pages that follow, He radiates as the Central Figure of a complex historical narrative about the Baha'i community of Washington, D.C. in the early decades of the twentieth century. He teaches and nurtures a diverse assemblage of souls as they struggle to realize the unifying vision of the Baha'i Faith in the context of an American social structure riven by the corrosion of racial prejudice.

Those who would follow the footsteps of 'Abdu'l-Bahá as they tread a path toward justice and racial equality will deeply appreciate this rendering of the early years of the Washington, D.C. Baha'i community. The authors of this slim volume have provided us a "thick history," in which frailty and missteps are constituent strands of a narrative that is ultimately about the courage and heroism of souls learning how to build a diverse, unified community. The story told in these pages is instructional and inspiring. But, most importantly, it is a story that is still unfolding.

Derik Smith, PhD,
Claremont Mckenna College

Chapter 1

"Look at Me, Follow Me, Be as I Am"

At the hour of dawn on May 29th, 1892, Baha'u'llah, the "Glory of God," ascended.

Over the next days, Shi'i and Sunni Muslims, Christians, Jews and Druze, clerics and poets, rich and poor, all came to grieve, a grief shared even more intensely by the thousands of His believers in Persia, India, Russia, Iraq, Turkey, Palestine, Egypt, and Syria. Tributes in poetry and prose in Turkish and Arabic poured in from cities around the Near East.[1]

On the ninth day after Baha'u'llah's passing, the *Book of the Covenant*, which was His Will and Testament, was read aloud before nine assembled witnesses and later that day before a larger gathering of family members, pilgrims, and local believers. In it, He reminds His followers:

> O ye that dwell on earth! The religion of God is for love and unity; make it not the cause of enmity or dissension. In the eyes of men of insight and the beholders of the Most Sublime Vision, whatsoever are the effective means for safeguarding and promoting the happiness and welfare of the children of men have already been revealed by the Pen of Glory. [2]

Then He makes a Covenant with them. He calls on them to turn to His son, 'Abdu'l-Baha, as the embodiment of this Covenant, the source of authority to whom all should turn, and the sole interpreter of the Word of God:

When the ocean of My presence hath ebbed and the Book of My Revelation is ended, turn your faces toward Him Whom God hath purposed, Who hath branched from this Ancient Root.' The object of this sacred verse is none other except the Most Mighty Branch ['Abdu'l-Baha].[3]

This Covenant, unique in history, has a power that is "the pivot of the oneness of mankind" and quickens and promotes "the development of all created things on earth,"[4] and it flows through the person, the words, and the actions of 'Abdu'l-Baha to whose example all could look for guidance. This Covenant was the "Sure Handle," "the light of the world," and "the educator of the minds, the spirits, the hearts and souls of men."[5]

Baha'u'llah gives this assurance at the end of the Book of His Covenant:

> That which is conducive to the regeneration of the world and the salvation of the peoples and kindreds of the earth hath been sent down from the heaven of the utterance of Him Who is the Desire of the world. Give ye a hearing ear to the counsels of the Pen of Glory. Better is this for you than all that is on the earth. Unto this beareth witness My glorious and wondrous Book.[6]

On the shores of Lake Michigan, amid the massive Chicago World's Fair of 1893 that showcased the latest in technological innovation, thought, art, music, and culture, the Parliament of the World's Religions—the first formal interfaith gathering in history—was held.[7] There, on September 23rd, 1893, the name of Baha'u'llah was mentioned for the first time in the United States. A paper written by the Rev. Henry Jessup was read by Rev. George Ford. Jessup's article begins with a condemnation of the exploitation of the peoples of Africa by Europeans and then pleads for the spread of Christian values to counter those of militarism and

Rev. Henry Jessup   Rev. George Ford

materialism which would turn the U.S. and Britain "into a double-headed monster of war and ambition."[8]

The true Christian mission is:

> That we who are made in the image of God should remember that all men are made in God's image. To this divine knowledge we owe all we are, all we hope to be, all we hope for. We are rising gradually toward that image and we owe to our fellow-men to aid them in returning to it in the glory of God.[9]

The author finishes his argument for true Christianity by using the example of Baha'u'llah and quoting His words:

> ... there died a few months ago since a famous Persian sage... named Beha Allah—the "Glory of God"— ... gave utterance to sentiments so noble, so Christlike that we repeat them as our closing words, that all nations should become one in faith, and all men as brothers: that the bonds of affection and unity between the sons of men should be strengthened; that the diversity of race be annulled. What harm is there in this? Yet so it shall be. These fruitless strifes, these ruinous wars

shall pass away, and the "most great peace" shall come.[10]

Attending the World's Fair in a business capacity was Anton Haddad, the first Baha'i to come to the United States. The interest in the ideas of Baha'u'llah generated at the Parliament of the World's Religions convinced Haddad's friend and business partner, Dr. Kheiralla, to set up classes. He found many people who were seeking and open to learning about this new spiritual message.

Among them was Thornton Chase, now considered the first American Baha'i, who had read Baha'u'llah's words in the article from the Parliament of Religions. Within a few years, several hundred people had taken these classes and heard the message. From these individuals came the nucleus of the Baha'i community in the United States, a committed and passionate band of believers.

By 1898, a group of American Baha'is decided that the time

Dr. Ibrahim Kheiralla   Anton Haddad

had come to make a pilgrimage to the Holy Land to learn directly from the Master as 'Abdu'l-Baha was commonly referred to out of respect though He himself preferred 'servant'—'Abdu'l. The trip was made possible by the generosity of Phoebe Hearst, a well-to-do heiress from California who had become a Baha'i.

Back row, L to R: Robert Turner; Anne Apperson (niece of Phoebe Apperson Hearst); Julia Pearson (Mrs. Hearst's assistant). Front row, L to R: Nabiha, daughter of Ibrahim Kheiralla; Mrs. Marion Kheiralla; Ibrahim Kheiralla; Lua Getsinger; Labiba, second daughter of Ibrahim Kheiralla.

Meeting 'Abdu'l-Baha in person opened the eyes of the American pilgrims to the spiritual reality taught by the Faith. He dispelled their mistaken notions by revealing to them its deeper truths. For three days and nights, the Master spoke of God and godliness, filling their hearts with understanding and firing their spirits with devotion to this new Revelation. They were being called to a far higher station than they had ever imagined.

'Abdu'l-Baha told them that if they arose to serve this great Cause with firm and steadfast faith, nothing was impossible:

> . . . I say unto you that anyone who will rise in the Cause of God at this time shall be filled with the spirit of God, and that He will send His hosts from heaven to help you, and that nothing shall be impossible to you if you have faith. And now I give you a commandment which shall be for a covenant between

you and Me — that ye have faith; that your faith be steadfast
as a rock that no storms can move, that nothing can disturb,
and that it endure through all things even to the end. . . . As ye
have faith so shall your powers and blessings be. This is the
balance — this is the balance — this is the balance.[11]

The very air in the Holy Land, scented with the perfume of orange
and rose blossoms, seemed to pilgrims to be filled with spiritual
power.

One of the fifteen pilgrims was a man who worked for Hearst,
Robert Turner, the first Black American to become a Baha'i. At the
Hearst home, he heard conversations about the Baha'i Faith and
became a believer himself. One evening during the pilgrimage,
the pilgrims gathered with 'Abdu'l-Baha in a room but Turner
stood outside feeling unworthy of being in the presence of the
Master and being from a society where people of different races
did not mix socially. Not seeing Turner, 'Abdu'l-Baha rose and
stepped out of the room where He saw Turner and embraced him
and insisted that he come and join the others.

Before the pilgrims returned to the United States, the Master
gave them one more powerful commandment without which
their efforts would not be blessed:

Another commandment I give unto you, that ye love one
another even as I love you. Great mercy and blessings are
promised to the people of your land, but on one condition:
that their hearts are filled with the fire of love, that they live
in perfect kindness and harmony like one soul in different
bodies. If they fail in this condition the great blessings will be
deferred. Never forget this; look at one another with the eye of
perfection; look at Me, follow Me, be as I am; take no thought
for yourselves or your lives, whether ye eat or whether ye
sleep, whether ye are comfortable, whether ye are well or ill,
whether ye are with friends or foes, whether ye receive praise
or blame; for all of these things ye must care not at all. Look at

Me and be as I am; ye must die to yourselves and to the world, so shall ye be born again and enter the Kingdom of Heaven. Behold a candle how it gives its light. It weeps its life away drop by drop in order to give forth its flame of light.[12]

Charlotte E. Brittingham Dixon was one of those waiting souls who found the Faith in Chicago. Raised in Arcadia, an estate three miles from Princess Anne, on Maryland's Eastern Shore, she grew up a spiritually sensitive child whose father was interested in Adventism, a Christian belief that the return of Jesus Christ was imminent. He attended meetings of the Millerites—as they were then known when he was a young man. Shunned by the churches, Millerites had to meet in the local courthouse in Princess Anne.

Charlotte attended the Washington Academy, an excellent private school in Princess Anne, then taught there for fourteen years. She married George Dixon on April 8, 1874; their first child, Louise, was born almost ten months later. George died suddenly in October 1877, and Charlotte gave their second daughter, who was only four months old, the name of "George" in memory of him.

Though she attended church regularly, she felt an undefinable spiritual thirst, a feeling that intensified as her daughters neared adulthood.

Her heart was open when she encountered the Baha'i Faith during the late summer of 1897 in Chicago:

In the year 1896, when I was forty-five years old, I had a most extraordinary experience in my religious life. Through my devotions, I received the Baptism of the Holy Spirit, known in the Churches as 'Sanctification', and it burst upon me in marvelous visions and words of fire.

During a period of three memorable months, I was in an exalted state of illumination and inexpressible rapture—each day I was shown mysteries, and the Bible became an open Book, as its meaning was made plain to me. Through visions and voices I was shown that a New Dispensation had dawned, and that Our Lord was again upon earth, to establish the glorious reign of Peace, and the Millennium. This was 1896.

I could not speak of this experience in this quiet town, as no one would understand it, but I prayed most earnestly for guidance, and light, and God opened a door for me, by taking me to live in Chicago, where I remained part of two years. While there I was wonderfully impressed that someone there knew of the great Revelation that had been shown me in Maryland.

In the late summer of 1897, I returned to Maryland for a visit, and before leaving Chicago, I besought God most earnestly, often lying on my face on the floor, that I should not be allowed to leave Chicago, without finding someone who knew of this Revelation. One day, while I was supplicating on my face, on the floor, a woman rang the doorbell asking for something, and I invited her to come in the apartment and be refreshed, as the heat was extreme: 'Be not forgetful to entertain strangers, for thereby some have entertained angels unaware.' While conversing with this stranger, she said to me, 'You should go to see Mrs. Reed, who is a good woman working in the slums with Mr. Moody'. I felt at once that I must try to see Mrs. Reed, and called upon her that afternoon, and was informed that she was out of the city.

I called again the following day and again the third day, but failed to find her. When I called the third day, a lady responded from the second floor, and when I asked for Mrs. Reed and questioned about her work, she paused a moment and then said: 'Woman, God sent you here; you are not seeking Mrs. Reed. We have the greatest message since Christ.'

She was a Physician of Chicago and had recently heard and accepted the Baha'i Revelation, and through our tears we conversed about it. She said she was unworthy to speak of the great Message, but referred me to a man from Palestine who was in Chicago giving the Baha'i Teachings to the first class of students in America, at that time. I lost no time in finding this man who had a class of about fifty earnest seekers. He told me the great Message, and I returned to Maryland in a few weeks, the first person on Maryland soil who knew of the Revelation.[13]

This "man from Palestine" was Dr. Kheiralla, and the experience with Mrs. Reed opened her spiritual eyes. Dixon accepted the Faith wholeheartedly on September 29, 1897, and she wasted no time introducing the Baha'i Faith to her relatives in Princess Anne:

> ... I taught my family, and they accepted it in a surprising way. My father died in the faith, receiving a glorious Baptism of the Spirit, and my brothers and sisters became Baha'is.[14]

Six of her family members in all accepted the new teaching.[15] Not stopping there, Dixon introduced the Faith to her relatives in Philadelphia who became quite interested, beginning a ripple that reached many waiting souls.[16]

She wrote to her brother, James Francis Brittingham, and his wife, Isabella Davis Brittingham, encouraging them to go attend Dr. Kheiralla's classes in New York. The Brittinghams were both deeply rooted in biblical prophecy and staunch members of their Episcopal Church and were convinced that Baha'u'llah was the returned Christ. They both became Baha'i in 1898.[17] In the coming years, Isabella ardently taught the Faith and helped her fellow believers gain a true understanding of it due to her own spiritual insight and what she learned during her pilgrimage to the Holy Land. She wrote an essay in which she described the station of the Master as being the Center of the Covenant, "He who knows no station save that of servitude, humility, and lowliness to the Beloved of El-Baha."[18]

In 1898, her sister-in-law, Charlotte Dixon, aflame with the same devotion, moved to the nation's capital, becoming the first Baha'i to settle in Washington, D.C.

Notes

1.   Shoghi Effendi, *God Passes By*, 238.
2.   Baha'u'llah, "Kitab-i-'Ahd," *Tablets*, 220.
3.   Ibid., 221.
4.   Shoghi Effendi, *God Passes By*, 238.
5.   Ibid., 239-40.
6.   Baha'u'llah, "Kitab-i-'Ahd," *Tablets*, 223.
7.   "World's Parliament of Religions."
8.   "Henry H. Jessup makes an Eloquent and Instructive Address," *The Inter Ocean*. September 24, 1893, 2.
9.   Ibid.
10. Ibid.
11. May Maxwell, *An Early Pilgrimage*, 40.
12. Ibid., 41-42.
13. Robert Stockman, *The Baha'i Faith in America*, vol. 1, 118-20.
14. Ibid., 120.
15. The six were her father William J. Brittingham; her brother, Henry Brittingham, Sr.; her sister, Laura V. Dixon; her sister's husband (who was also her own husband's brother), Thomas Dixon; and her niece, the daughter of Laura and Thomas (Ibid., 128-29).
16. Charlotte Dixon's daughter, Louise Dixon, and her sister, Henrietta Brittingham, both resided in Philadelphia and became quite interested in the Baha'i Faith. About twenty Philadelphians became Baha'is with the teaching of Mrs. Sarah Herron, a former Chicago resident sponsored by the Brittingham sisters to teach them (Ibid., 129).
17. This was the first class in New York City on the Baha'i Faith. There were three families who attended the classes in Chicago and wanted to learn more: the Dodges, the Hoars, and the Talbots. Isabella Brittingham remembers three others becoming Baha'is at the end of those classes: Margaret Stone, Marietta Ball, and Margaret Kern. The class ran from February to March 1898 (Ibid., 121).
18. Isabella Brittingham, "The Revelation of Baha'ullah," quoted in Whitehead, *Early Baha'is*, 132.

Mirza Abu'l-Fazl, painted by D.C. Baha'i Alice Pike Barney

Chapter 2

Mirza Abu'l Fazl and Early Conversions

O nce she'd set up residence in Washington, Charlotte Dixon
immediately set about teaching the lessons she had only just
received herself from Dr. Kheiralla. Soon, she had brought into
being a nascent Bahá'í community. By September 1899, there were
at least seven Bahá'ís in the District of Columbia. Filled with enthusiasm, she vigorously proclaimed the new teachings throughout her own social network of prominent Washingtonians.

The fledgling community gained much strength with the
arrival of several knowledgeable and strong Bahá'ís who were
known and respected members of the local society—Phoebe
Hearst,[1] the widow of a United States Senator; Mason Remey,[2]
born into a prominent naval family; and Laura Barney, active and
well-known in D.C. social and artistic circles.[3]

'Abdu'l-Bahá guided these emerging, small, scattered communities in the United States through constant letter writing and
the sending of teachers, none of whom was more distinguished
than the great Bahá'í scholar, Mirza Abu'l-Fazl.

Mirza Abu'l-Fazl first encountered the Bahá'í Faith in the
form of an illiterate blacksmith in whose workshop he stopped
one day. This unlearned man asked the scholar about an Islamic
tradition in the form of a syllogism. Was it true that an angel accompanied every drop of rain as it fell to the ground? Abu'l-Fazl
agreed. Was it true that if there was a dog in a house, no angel
would ever visit it? Abu'l-Fazl—before having the time to think
of how the two statements were connected—agreed again. Then,

Phoebe Hearst, titled "Mother of the Faithful" by 'Abdu'l-Baha

Laura Dreyfus Barney

the blacksmith concluded, no rain would ever fall on a house with a dog in it. Abu'l-Fazl was shocked and ashamed of having been led to agreeing to a completely illogical statement. After hearing that this humble man who had bested him was a Bahá'í, he sought other Bahá'ís. He read from the Writings of Bahá'u'lláh that contained prophecies for events that were to unfold in their time. When these prophecies came to pass, he declared that he believed Bahá'u'lláh was the new Manifestation of God.

Abu'l-Fazl suffered greatly for becoming a Bahá'í. He was let go from being the head of a religious college and imprisoned for months at a time on three different occasions for teaching the new religion. Nevertheless, he arose with great fervor to spread the new message. Throughout Iran, Turkmenistan, and Egypt, Abu'l-Fazl taught the Faith to many Muslims, Zoroastrians, and Jews, and so high was the respect in which he was held and so convincing the arguments and proofs from the deep well of his knowledge that many converted.[4]

Obedient to the wishes of 'Abdu'l-Bahá, he undertook the long journey to the United States. He left behind in Egypt his extensive library, his students, and his scholarly projects and boarded a ship to cross a vast ocean to what was for him a completely foreign land.

The Bahá'ís greeted him with great warmth and respect, but they could not truly understand him. They knew little to nothing of the great body of theological and philosophical knowledge in which he had worked his whole life, nor had they read much of the Bahá'í Writings, little of which had yet been translated into English. Abu'l-Fazl found himself alone in Washington, D.C., braving cold weather and foreign food, not speaking the language or understanding the customs. His Near Eastern clothing of long robes attracted the unwanted attention of neighborhood boys who followed and harassed him by throwing projectiles at him such that he had to move to another rooming house.

But 'Abdu'l-Bahá had asked him to undertake this teaching mission and so, being fully aware of the Master's true station, he rose to the occasion despite these hardships. His major project was to write a book to help Western Bahá'ís gain a much greater understanding of the Bahá'í teachings so that the communities could grow and flourish. The result of his effort was *The Bahá'í Proofs*, the only Bahá'í book of this early period to be reprinted later in the century such was its enduring value.

The first half of the book provided an overview of the Writings of the Báb and Bahá'u'lláh, an explanation of the Bábi-Bahá'í calendar, and an in-depth discussion of several Bahá'í social principles, all of which were new to the Bahá'ís at that time. The purpose of the second half, written at the specific request of 'Abdu'l-Bahá, was to lay the foundation for understanding the Advent of Bahá'u'lláh in terms of the Bahá'í Writings and previous Revelations. Abu'l-Fazl covered the prophecies of the Abrahamic religions to show that the Day of Judgement had come. He explained the nature of God and the need for a Manifestation, and he set forth the proofs for recognizing the Manifestation of God which are the existence of a revelation, the power of the Word of its Scriptures to transform lives, miracles, and the fulfillment of prophecy. Some aspects of all of these existed in the past but in Bahá'u'lláh, these proofs were fully realized.[5]

Mirza Abu'l-Fazl based his arguments entirely on the Aristotelean logic and Islamic philosophy in which he was steeped. He did not make appeals to everyday ideas of common sense or popular opinions. This rigor was lost on American Bahá'ís who preferred their vague ideas of mundane spirituality such as the interpretation of dreams. Still, the book helped to introduce the early Bahá'ís to basic Bahá'í concepts about which they had previously been unaware.[6]

Mason Remey, a prominent early American Bahá'í, referred to Abu'l-Fazl as "the real pioneer teacher to America,"[7] because in addition to this important book, Abu'l-Fazl, speaking through the diplomat and interpreter Ali Kuli Khan,[8] held regular classes that drew hundreds and at which many came to believe in the Bahá'í Faith. Among the most notable for the growth of the Bahá'í community was a spiritually sensitive and insightful young woman who guided her entire family into the Faith: Pauline Hannen.

Pauline Knobloch Hannen was the youngest daughter of Karl Knobloch, an architect from Germany, and Amalie Knobloch. Both were devout members of the Free Lutheran Church. Karl moved the family to the United States to pursue a professional opportunity. Two of her siblings, her sisters Fanny and Alma, survived childhood but the others—Ida, Paul, and Bruno—did not; her older brother, Karl, died when she was twenty.[9] At fourteen, she lost her father, and the bereaved family moved back to Washington, D.C. from North Carolina. She met and married Joseph Hannen, a young man from Virginia who moved to D.C. with his mother some years after his father left "to get milk" for baby Joseph and never returned.[10] The couple had two sons, Carl and Paul, and a daughter, Gladys, but she died in infancy.

Joseph was working for Viavi, a company that made health products, when one day he began to train a new employee, Sarah Etta Sargent. During a conversation about spiritual powers, she mentioned that she knew a Mrs. Jones who could "accomplish wonderful things through prayer, and who could also tell me about a most interesting religious movement."[11] She invited Joseph and Pauline to visit her.

One stormy October Saturday evening in 1902, Joseph and Pauline, and her sisters, made their way to the home of Mrs. Jones, "a dark olive complexioned lady possessing a sturdy figure." After prayers and a presentation, they were invited to return the following Sunday and meet her friends. Fanny was impressed that "that lady's God is a living reality, not something ethereal or off at a great distance, but a *living reality*."[12]

The four did not go to their respective church duties the next day and instead, returned to Mrs. Jones. There they heard "some beautiful teachings from the Orient" followed by silent prayer.

Pauline Hannen, titled "Pioneer of Race Unity in America" by Hand of the Cause of God Mr. Louis George Gregory

After leaving, Fanny expressed her concern that they did not "want to get mixed up in this Orientalism."[13]

Pauline though was interested in Sargent's offer to "visit a wonderful teacher from Persia." She was, like her sister, concerned about "this Oriental," but her "love for the Truth was greater than my fear of man,"[14] so she went, bringing her mother Amalie along. Meeting Mirza Abu'l-Fazl and hearing the Message changed her completely:

> At three o'clock, Monday, Nov. 24, I received a Message from this venerable Teacher, through his interpreter, Mirza Ali Kuli Khan, that completely changed my whole life; from that hour on I was a new creature.
>
> After giving me wonderful answers to my questions, I was told in a straightforward manner that Christ had returned, that the world at large rejected his claim just as the people always in times past had treated the Messengers of God. Although Mirza Ali Kuli Khan went on with proof and argument I heard nothing, only the words ringing in my ears. 'Christ has come again in the flesh.'[15]

Pauline was overwhelmed by what she heard. For the next few days and nights, "storms of thought raged through my being," and "hell itself could not compare to the agony of my soul." She offered "such a prayer as I had never known in my life, begging for sight." She earnestly pleaded for her family to join her at Laura Barney's home on Wednesday to hear Abu'l-Fazl. There, she felt this "unutterable joy that flooded me on that memorable afternoon," and "her happy heart sang out."[16] That Wednesday, as it turned out, was November 26th, the "birthday" of 'Abdu'l-Bahá, now known as the Day of the Covenant.[17]

She endeavored to teach her family members—all of whom were active churchgoers—the new Faith. She was patient but persistent: "I became a nuisance to them all."[18]

Her mother marveled at how much she spoke of the Faith as

she had never spoken much at all. She said: "Now you seem to have been aroused, as out of a sleep, into a fluent speaker. When you talk, I can see. When you are absent, doubt assails me."[19]

Alma was busy with her work as a seamstress, so Pauline went to her work and spoke at some length about the Glad Tidings of Bahá'u'lláh while her sister and "a light-colored, intelligent, seamstress, Pocahontas Pope" listened. Finally, Alma had to say: "My cup is full. It can contain no more. Please stop now."[20]

Alma fell into ill health due to a personal setback in her life and went to Europe to try to improve her condition and spirits. After she returned, Pauline came to see her. She had started to attend the sessions at the home of Mrs. Jones and was eager to share the good news of Bahá'u'lláh. Alma remembers that: "Trembling and with emotion she told me that the Lord was on Earth and in Prison and some more details." She was concerned that her younger sister had "Become over nervous"[21] and caressed her and spoke to her gently.

Pauline came to see Alma again, this time bringing with her a prayer for healing that she wanted her sister to have:

O my God! Thy name is my healing. Thy Remembrance is my remedy. Thy nearness is my hope. Thy love is my joyous companion, and Thy Mercy is my refuge in this world and in the worlds to come. Verily Thou art the Giver, the All-Knowing, the Wise.[22]

Pauline passed the prayer over to her sister with a pleading and affectionate expression asking that when she use it, she read it nine times. Alma was moved by her sister's sincerity. Even though Alma had been a Bible teacher and active in charitable organizations, this direct and intimate personal appeal moved her.

When Alma said the healing prayer, she felt ". . . such a strong spiritual vibration passing through my entire body. . ." that she realized that she ". . . heretofore not prayed at all, in fact had only repeated words." She began attending the prayer sessions at the home of Mrs. Jones where a small group gathered around the hearth of the home and ". . . like detached souls. The words they read from Bahá'u'lláh seemed powerful and their prayers vibrating that Spirit for which we all crave."[23] She also began going to the talks of Abu'l-Fazl, which Ali Kuli Khan interpreted, and studying the Bahá'í Writings well into the night. The participants brought notebooks to write down Abu'l-Fazl's explanations of the prophecies of the Bible that were fulfilled by the Bahá'í Revelation. He encouraged Alma to incorporate these ideas and the mention of Bahá'u'lláh and 'Abdu'l-Bahá into the Bible class she taught.

After she was confirmed in her belief, Alma wrote a letter to 'Abdu'l-Bahá, as was the custom of new Bahá'ís at the time, in which she asked for the interpretation of a dream she'd had. The Master wrote to her:

> . . . As to that great Sun which thou sawest in a dream: That is His Holiness the Promised One and the lights thereof are His bounties. The surface of the water is transparent body—that is, pure hearts. Its waves are the moving of the hearts, the cheering of the souls—that is the spiritual feelings and merciful sentiments. Thank thou God for that thou hast had such a revelation in the world of dreams.[24]

'Abdu'l-Bahá also explained that:

> . . . thanksgiving for the bounty of the Merciful One consists in the illumination of the heart and the feeling of the soul. This is the reality of thanksgiving. But although offering thanks through speech or writings is approvable, yet, in comparison with that, it is but unreal, for the foundation is spiritual feeling and merciful sentiments.[25]

Fanny was the most hesitant of the sisters to engage in the study of the Bahá'í Faith. Pauline visited her every Sunday to talk with her about the teachings, especially the prophecies of the Bible and how these were fulfilled by Bahá'u'lláh's Coming. Though this subject could be of great interest to Bible-based Christians, for Fanny, "the constant conversation dealing with religion became quite trying to me. . ."

But then one day, Fanny was participating in a Bible class that included Jesus's multiplication of the loaves and the fishes. One of the parishioners suggested that this may have been a case in which Jesus had hypnotized the multitude into believing they were eating loaves and fishes by using 'mesmerism', a form of hypnosis that was popular in those days. The silliness of this suggestion offended Fanny's deep spiritual beliefs. Sometime later, Pauline came to visit after she had attended a talk by Abu'l-Fazl in which they had discussed just such miracles from the Bible. Abu'l-Fazl had explained that while it was good to feed people for one afternoon: "How much more wonderful is it to know that He fed the multitudes with the Bread of Life for nineteen hundred years, and baskets of crumbs that were gathered, you Christians are living today!"[26] This profound insight into the Scripture was the "turning point"[27] for Fanny in her journey towards the Faith.

Joseph Hannen did not need much persuasion. From the moment Pauline began to tell him about the Faith and its teachings, he was touched by its spirit: "never since it came to me have I resisted its power, tho' it was long ere I could claim enough of its spiritual influx to call myself a follower."[28]

With Pauline's loving persistence and Abu'l-Fazl's great knowledge, Pauline, the youngest of the family, could write that "each member of my family received the light of Truth in his own way. . ."[29]

O God! Grant Washington happiness and peace! Illuminate that land with the light of the faces of the friends, make it a paradise of Glory, let it become an envy of the green gardens of the earth! Help the friends, increase their number, make their hearts sources of inspiration and their souls dawnings of light. Thus may that city become a beautiful paradise and fragrant with the fragrance of musk."³⁰

'Abdu'l-Bahá blessed the Bahá'ís of Washington with this prayer of encouragement that they might inspire others and "increase their numbers." To Joseph Hannen, the Master wrote that they must "never stain themselves with the world" nor accept "the least pecuniary reward" but they should strive to "associate with all people" because "freely have they received" and so, "freely should they give the Glad Tidings."³¹

Though written to Hannen, these words applied to all the Bahá'ís. Their mission was to bring the news of Bahá'u'lláh's Revelation to all people like flames giving off light or clouds nourishing the soil with rain.

They had an example in Mirza Abu'l-Fazl who taught the Faith to many despite all the hardships he'd experienced. He did this for no other reason than his love and respect for 'Abdu'l-Bahá. He wanted nothing for himself and even emphasized to students not to accept his interpretations but only those of the Master.

In addition to Abu'l-Fazl, the capacity of the Bahá'í community of D.C. to grow was developed by another teacher sent by 'Abdu'l-Bahá, Ahmad Sohrab, as well as the writing of in-depth and accurate pamphlets on the Faith by Mason Remey, the publication of the Tablets of 'Abdu'l-Bahá, and, in 1908, of *Some Answered Questions*, initiated by Laura Barney and one of the most important repositories of the wisdom of 'Abdu'l-Bahá.

The new Message—as the Bahá'ís of D.C. would soon learn—was universal. It was one thing to believe in this as an idea, it was a whole other thing to make it a reality. The new Message was not only for those who were in their same social circles.

But this was a society deeply segregated by, among other things, race. For these early Bahá'ís, who were all white, to go beyond what was familiar required of them a supreme effort, not at all in conformity with the established norms of the society in which they lived and moved.

Pauline Hannen began this effort right in her own home with her washerwoman, Carrie York, and her sister's seamstress, Pocahontas Pope.

Notes

1. Phoebe Hearst moved to Washington, D.C. from California because her
    husband George, who made his money in mining, was elected senator.
    She gave generously to educational institutions, including the first
    free kindergarten, the University of California, and a teacher training
    school, among many others. She founded the National Cathedral
    School for Girls in Washington, D.C. in 1900, and the National Congress
    of Mothers, the forerunner of the modern PTA, in 1897. Hearst died in
    California in 1919. She became a Bahá'í in 1898 and went on the first pil-
    grimage of Western Bahá'ís to 'Abdu'l-Bahá in Palestine. Of those days,
    she wrote "Altho my stay in 'Acca was very short, as I was there only
    three days, yet I assure you those three days were the most memorable
    days of my life, still I feel incapable of describing them in the slightest
    degree." (Hearst, "Two letters," 801).
2. Charles Mason Remey became a Bahá'í in Paris in 1899. Returning to
    the United States, he actively taught the Bahá'í Faith as a travelling
    teacher both nationally and internationally throughout Europe and
    Asia, and by writing pamphlets and essays. Interested in architecture,
    he designed the houses of worship in Uganda and in Australia as
    well as drawing up plans for others. In addition to his Bahá'í work, he
    wrote hundreds of volumes of memoirs, correspondence, and diaries
    and other personal work. He was appointed by Shoghi Effendi as the
    President of the International Bahá'í Council and then, as a Hand of
    the Cause. After the passing of Shoghi Effendi, he came to believe and
    claimed that he should be the next Head of the Faith and attempted to
    wrest control of the Faith. His claims were rejected, and he was expelled
    from the community (Stockman, "Remey, Charles Mason").
3. Moe, *Aflame with Devotion*, 15. Laura Barney was the daughter of Alice
    Pike Barney, later Hemnick. Alice Barney built the family home, Studio
    House, which hosted 'Abdu'l-Bahá several times and was the site of
    Bahá'í activities and artistic and social evenings. Her mother came from
    a family of wealthy industrialists and being highly creative herself, used
    her money as a patroness of the arts. Laura went to school in France
    and studied theater and sculpture in Paris where she first heard of the
    Bahá'í Faith from May Bolles (later Maxwell). Sensitive, imaginative,
    and idealistic, she accepted the teachings right away and went to the
    Holy Land with a pilgrimage group. She served the Faith actively and
    later married Hippolyte Dreyfus, the first Frenchman to become a
    Bahá'í. She made several pilgrimages to 'Abdu'l-Bahá between 1904-0
    6 and during those, she asked 'Abdu'l-Bahá a series of questions over
    lunches which she then had recorded by his secretaries. These an-
    swers were later verified by 'Abdu'l-Bahá and translated into English.

Hippolyte Dreyfus later translated them into French. *Some Answered Questions*, the title given to 'Abdu'l-Bahá's 'table talks,' were published in English and Persian in 1908 (Khademi, "Glimpses into the Life").

4. Stockman, *The Bahá'í Faith in America*, v. 2, 80-81.
5. Ibid., 86.
6. Moe, *Aflame with Devotion*, 22.
7. Charles Mason Remey, quoted in Stockman, *The Bahá'í Faith in America*, v. 2, 86.
8. Ali Kuli Khan was an Iranian Bahá'í who was the Chargé d'Affaires at the Persian Consulate. He translated for Mirza Abu'l-Fazl during the scholar's time in the United States. He did many early translations of the Bahá'í Writings. He married Florence Breed, an American Bahá'í from Boston. Their union was one of the first intercultural marriages in the American Bahá'í community. Khan served for years on Bahá'í institutions in the United States including the Bahá'í Temple Unity board and the National Spiritual Assembly of the Bahá'ís of the United States ("Ali Kuli Khan").
9. Stockman, "Knobloch, Fanny."
10. Moe, *Aflame with Devotion*, 39.
11. Joseph Hannen, quoted in ibid., 19.
12. Fanny Knobloch, quoted in ibid., 31.
13. Fanny Knobloch, quoted in ibid..
14. Pauline Hannen, quoted in ibid., 21.
15. Ibid.
16. 'Abdu'l-Bahá was born the same day as the Báb declared Himself to be the Manifestation of God (May 23, 1844). In His humility, 'Abdu'l-Bahá did not allow Bahá'ís to celebrate his birthday but instead chose a day that was the furthest on the calendar from the Báb's Declaration, showing the great distance in Station between Himself and the Báb. Neither was that chosen day to be a birthday for him, but a celebration of the Covenant of God of which He was the embodiment.
17. Pauline Hannen quoted in Moe, *Aflame with Devotion*, 21.
18. Pauline Hannen, quoted in in ibid., 23.
19. Pauline Hannen, quoted in in ibid..
20. Alma Knobloch, quoted in in ibid., 23.
21. Bahá'u'lláh, quoted in in ibid., 24-25. This is the "Healing Prayer" as it was translated at the time—1903; it should be considered a historical document. Tablets of 'Abdu'l-Bahá identified as 'historical documents' are English translations that were prepared at the time the Tablet was revealed and sent to the recipient together with the original Tablet. These are not authorized translations and their accuracy has not been verified.

22. Alma Knobloch, quoted in ibid., 25.
23. 'Abdu'l-Bahá, *Tablets of 'Abdu'l-Bahá, vol. II*, letter to Alma Knobloch, quoted in Moe, *Aflame with Devotion*, 27.
24. Ibid.
25. Mirza Abu'l-Fazl, quoted in a letter from Fannie Knobloch, quoted in ibid., 33.
26. Fannie Knobloch, quoted in ibid., 33.
27. Joseph Hannen, quoted in ibid., 20.
28. Pauline Hannen, quoted in ibid,, 24.
29. Abdu'l-Baha Abbas, *Tablets*, 730.
30. Letter of 'Abdu'l-Bahá to Joseph Hannen, quoted in Moe, *Aflame with Devotion*, 50.
31. Sohrab served as one of the secretaries of 'Abdu'l-Bahá for the next seven years (authors' note).

Chapter 3

Black and White
in the Nation's Capital

On land formerly settled by the Nacostine at the confluence of the Potomac and Anacostia Rivers, English colonists developed large tobacco plantations worked by enslaved people brought from Africa, and the town of Washington rose.

From its very beginning, the city of Washington was both the capital of a Republic, the first in the West in many centuries, and a fully functioning slave society, a moral contradiction embedded in the fabric of the nation.

In the late 1700s, slave labor was used along with European workers to build the Capitol building of the new nation and the President's official residence, the White House. The enslavers "rented" out the labor they enslaved and then kept the profits. The use of this slave labor drove down the wages of the laborers for hire.[1] In 1800, seventy-five percent of men of European descent in the city were property-less laborers, mostly Irish, who'd fled the poverty of their homeland and struggled to get an economic foothold because they had to compete with free slave labor.

As the need for slave labor decreased with the decline of the area's tobacco industry, more Black Americans were able to purchase their freedom, and a free Black American society emerged. The percentage of enslaved people went from eighty-three percent in 1800 to forty-nine percent in 1830. Black Americans, both free and enslaved, were linked together through family bonds, churches, and social organizations. Attracted by opportunity, free Black migrants moved into Washington.

Enslaved workers passing the Capitol grounds, 1815, published in
A Popular History of the United States, 1876.

The top priority for free Black Americans was education.
Denied entry into the public "pauper" schools for whites, they
founded their own private ones with the help of free Black
and white donors. George Bell, Moses Liverpool, and Nicholas
Franklin, all formerly enslaved persons who had been deprived of
formal education, founded the first school for Black Americans,
the Bell School at 2nd St. and D St. S.E.

Free Black women found work primarily as domestics,
including being seamstresses, and free Black men as construc-
tion and maintenance workers in public projects and private
houses. A small professional class of free Black Washingtonians
emerged—teachers, ministers, business owners—and they began
buying property.

The emergence of a free Black society and its influence
on those still enslaved were of grave concern to the white city
leaders. They passed the first "black code" in the city, requiring
Black Americans to give "evidence" of their free status, imposing
a ten o'clock curfew, and prohibiting assembly in "a disorderly or
tumultuous manner."[2]

An active and lucrative slave trade continued in the city; by the 1820s, an entire city block was a holding pen used for the slave trading company,[3] Franklin and Armfield, which bought slaves from landowners in the region who were shifting their land to other crops. In this large structure, slaves waited in terror to learn their fate and board a vessel for their destination in the slave markets of the deep south.[4]

The company dressed the men, women, and children in clothes and fed them well enough to give the appearance of health to the slave traders who were plied with wine, cheese, and other niceties. The owners of this slave trading company sought to project a gentlemanly image; an English observer, though, described those who came to purchase people as "sordid, illiterate, and vulgar."[5]

Abolitionists also focused their efforts on D.C. where the everyday outrages of slavery could be easily seen. Privately owned "slave pens" were in full view including one right under the gaze of the Capitol. In these pens, Black people were held, beaten, and deprived of food and sleep before being sold on. Free Black Americans were in constant danger of being kidnapped off the streets or put into one of these pens if they lacked the "proper" documents. With the rise of a small but very vocal abolition movement, southern senators were determined to hold the line in D.C. as it was the capital city and, lacking political representation in Congress, it couldn't fight back. Tensions over slavery in D.C. continued to rise until the Compromise of 1850 was passed into law that banned the slave trade in D.C. in return for a stronger Fugitive Slave Act.

With the outbreak of the Civil War and the passing of the Emancipation Proclamation, the Republican-led Congress abolished the black codes, established a school system for Black children, and lifted restrictions for Black Americans on economic activities. D.C. was now even more of an attractive destination for Black migrants who made their way to this city in larger numbers than ever before. Black residents now used public spaces for all kinds of celebrations and commemorations. They pushed harder now for full access to education. White city leaders saw emancipation as the end of Black striving, not the beginning, and were worried by what they saw happening after the Civil War. One journalist noted that "if slavery is dead, its spirit is not."[6]

The Freedmen's Bureau helped to settle the numerous new Black migrants who had come to the city during the war. To placate white concerns about having Black people living near them or squatting on their unused lots, the Bureau created Black areas such as Barry's Farm which were set aside to be lived in by Black residents.

The Bureau also built numerous schools for Black children. By June of 1866, there were 10,000 Black children enrolled in schools in D.C. In March 1867, Congress passed a bill to create an integrated university in D.C. that focused on Black students. Howard University, named after Gen. Oliver Otis Howard, a Civil War hero who was both the founder of the university and, at the time, commissioner of the the head of the Bureau, became the leading Black university in the country.

In December of 1866, Congress passed a suffrage bill guaranteeing the right to vote to Black men. In Washington, D.C., a successful drive to register Black voters resulted in new Black office holders and a bi-racial city government. But just as the Reconstruction movement—the era from 1865-77 when the Federal government sought to reintegrate the Southern states into the Union and guarantee the rights of the newly 'freedmen'—lost steam in the nation, the advancement of Black Americans in the District was halted by the collapse of the Freedmen's Bank due to the Panic of 1873, corruption by city and white banking officials, and a return to direct rule by unelected commissioners appointed by Congress. The city, like the country, now followed an economic model of development that favored white elites.[7]

Compared to the rest of the country, D.C. still offered much to Black Americans in terms of economic, social, and educational opportunities as well as an escape from the worst of the racial violence that stalked the South—lynching. The Black population of D.C. grew seventy-four percent between 1870 and 1890. A vibrant intellectual and artistic life developed, and numerous civic institutions were formed such as the Bethel Literary and Historical Society, founded in 1882, where the important questions of the day were debated.[8]

Most Black Americans though had little hope for economic advancement. Three-quarters of Black Americans in the 1870s were unskilled or domestic workers. The city commissioners were all white, and they disregarded the grievances regarding employment opportunities for Black citizens and paid no attention to high poverty rates among Black Americans and their consequences. This situation also exacerbated class tensions among Black Americans, with wealthier families wanting to avoid association with poorer Black people and favoring lighter skinned individuals, reflecting the racial color values of the country.

With the end of Reconstruction in 1877, there was in D.C., as in the rest of the country, a retreat from the racial progress made in the years after the Civil War, which in the City's case meant giving up on biracial governance by eliminating self-rule. Without integrated politics, neighborhoods became increasingly segregated racially and economically even as its population boomed; the West End near Georgetown became one of the first exclusively white and well-to-do neighborhoods in the District.

In the late 1800s, Washington continued to attract Black migrants because as one migrant put it "Washington wasn't South." In the South, the years after Reconstruction saw the establishment of repressive Jim Crow laws, absolute segregation, debt peonage, and lynching. Meanwhile, the city's Black population during the last quarter of the 1800s grew by 45 percent.[9]

Nevertheless, Black men and women in D.C. made much less and had far fewer opportunities than their white counterparts. Ninty percent of Black women could only find work as domestics even if they were educated—"a kitchen is where a colored woman got work,"[10] as one woman put it. Jim Crow laws were passed in Maryland and Virginia, and, as Congress retreated from all the protections for Black citizens, segregation was mandated throughout the city. An anti-vagrancy law was passed with a broad definition of "vagrant" primarily aimed at the city's large Black population who were blamed by a South Carolina senator for criminality due to the "overeducation of some negroes who are made to have higher aspirations than it is possible for them to attain."[11]

The contrast between the nation's ideals and the racial realities was evident for all to see. As a Black educator wrote:

> Surely nowhere in the world do oppression and persecution based solely on the color of the skin appear more hateful and hideous than in the capital of the United States because the chasm between the principles upon which this Government was founded, in which it still professes to believe, and those which are daily practiced under the protection of the flag, yawns so wide and deep.[12]

During the late 1800s and the early 1900s, the city's Black neighborhoods continued to offer increasing opportunities for building wealth, the churches were a force for political and social organizing, and a great deal of effort was put into schools, such that they became the best Black schools in the country. Much in life, though, for Black Americans in D.C. remained more of "a promise than a fulfillment."[13]

Pauline Hannen grew up in North Carolina in a completely segregated society whose racial prejudice she unconsciously adopted:

> . . . when I was a little girl in Wilmington, N.C., teaching and environment had made me regard colored people with something like terror. I had known of the frightful retribution

visited by whites on negroes for offenses of which I assumed they must be guilty.[14]

Growing up in such an environment, she did not question her assumptions about race until she encountered the Bahá'í Writings in which she read:

> O Children of Men! Know ye not why We created you all from the same dust? That no one should exalt himself over the other. Ponder at all times in your hearts how ye were created. Since We have created you all from one same substance it is incumbent on you to be even as one soul, to walk with the same feet, eat with the same mouth, and dwell in the same land, that from your inmost being, by your deeds and actions, the signs of oneness and the essence of detachment may be made manifest. Such is My counsel to you, O concourse of light! Heed ye this counsel that ye may obtain the fruit of holiness from the tree of wondrous glory.[15]

This Scriptural passage opened her heart to the possibility that what she had known about race was fundamentally wrong. Then one wintry day she walked by a Black woman who was carrying several bundles and whose shoelaces were untied. To the astonishment of onlookers, Pauline knelt down and tied the woman's shoelaces and "from that moment was possessed with the conviction that I must create a work of brotherhood among the colored people. . ."[16]

Without hesitation, Pauline began teaching the Faith of Bahá'u'lláh to Black Americans. She began with where she was—her own household. Pauline called on the lady who worked as a washerwoman for her family, Ms. Carrie York, because "her true Christ spirit attracted me to her home as a good place to begin."[17] Those meetings at the York home were "the candle stick from which the Light was spread." Despite the strong social conventions against the free association of Black and white people, "to these classes came ministers and teachers" and, so keen was the interest that "the discussions crowded midnight." Even her husband, Joseph, who "disapproved of these adventures" and "expected the fire of zeal to burn itself out" became a "tireless worker in the same kind of service."[18]

Pauline's sister, Alma Knobloch, was also engaged in teaching the Faith to a Black woman in her household, Pocahontas Pope.[19] Pope was born and raised in North Carolina, the daughter of Mary (Kay) Sanling and John Kay. When she was eighteen years old, she married John Pope and moved to D.C. where he worked in the U.S. Census Office. Both were active in the Second Avenue Baptist Church, one of the oldest Black American congregations in the city. Pocahontas demonstrated an earnest religiosity.

After learning of the Faith from Alma, Pope began attending the gatherings in Carrie York's home. Soon, she decided to open her home to discussions on the Faith thus becoming "the second of our Washington houses of Faith." Her husband, John Pope, being well-versed in the Bible, asked many pertinent questions, adding greatly to the evenings. Pocahontas Pope became a confirmed Bahá'í and received the following from 'Abdu'l-Bahá:

> Render thanks to the Lord that among that race thou art the first believer, arisen to guide others It is my hope that through the bounties and favours of the Abhá beauty thy countenance may be illumined, thy disposition pleasing, and thy fragrance diffused, that thine eyes may be seeing, thine ears attentive, thy tongue eloquent, thy heart filled with supreme glad-tidings, and thy soul refreshed by divine fragrances, so that thou mayest arise among that race and occupy thyself with the edification of the people, and become filled with light. Although the pupil of the eye is black, it is the source of light. Thou shalt likewise be.[20]

The home of Ms. Rhoda Turner, a Black American woman, became the third one opened to the teaching of the new Faith. White

FIRST AFRICAN–AMERICAN
BAHA'I IN WASHINGTON, D.C.

POCAHONTAS
POPE

c1864   1938

RENDER THANKS TO THE LORD THAT
AMONG THAT RACE THOU ART THE FIRST
BELIEVER, ...ARISEN TO GUIDE OTHERS –
'ABDU'L-BAHA

A plaque honoring Pocahontas Pope at the National Harmony Memorial Park, replacing her headstone which had been dumped by the speculator Louis Bell as riprap into the Potomac River 80 miles south of Washington in 1960 when he purchased the DC Harmony Cemetery. The cemetery had been established in 1828 by the city's free African American population and transferred the bodies to the new cemetery.

believers attended as well, and white Bahá'ís such as Hooper Harris,[21] Howard McNutt, Lua Getsinger, Isabella Brittingham, Madame Dreyfus-Barney, and others, spoke. The new message aroused interest among Black Washingtonians and soon, there were fifteen Black American Bahá'ís in the District.[22]

One cold and blustery evening in late 1907, a man was making his way across the street in front of the Treasury Department to learn about the Bahá'í Faith. Across the street, in the Corona building, Pauline Hannen waited for seekers to come. She stood and greeted the tall lawyer when he walked in, telling him he would "hear something very wonderful, though difficult." Little did she know what a broad and powerful impact this man would have on the growth and development of the Bahá'í community. He introduced himself as Louis Gregory.

Notes

1. Asch and Musgrove, *Chocolate City*, 30-31.
2. Ibid., 45.
3. In those days, the city included today's Alexandria, Virginia, where Franklin and Armfield was located (Authors' note).
4. Ibid., 51.
5. Ibid., 48.
6. Ibid., 133.
7. Ibid., 168.
8. Ibid., 169.
9. Ibid., 206.
10. Ibid., 208.
11. Ibid., 209.
12. Mary Church Terrell, quoted in ibid., 209.
13. Paul Laurence Dunbar, quoted in ibid., 210.
14. Pauline Hannen quoted in Moe, *Aflame with Devotion*, 65.
15. Bahá'u'lláh, *The Hidden Words*, 65.
16. Pauline Hannen quoted in Moe, *Aflame with Devotion*, 66.
17. Pauline Hannen quoted in ibid., 66.
18. Pauline Hannen quoted in ibid., 67.
19. "Pocahontas Kay Grizzard Pope."
20. 'Abdu'l-Bahá quoted in Moe, *Aflame with Devotion*, 68.
21. A Bahá'í from New York who travelled extensively to teach the Bahá'í Faith and who served on the New York City Bahá'í Administrative Board (authors' note).
22. Moe, *Aflame with Devotion*, 68.

Louis Gregory as a young man, probably on graduating
from Fisk University, 1896.

Chapter 4

Louis Gregory and Agnes Parsons

My first information about the Revelation of Bahá'u'lláh came in the latter part of 1907, just thirty years ago. Mention of it came from one who might have been regarded as traditionally foe. At the time I was a Federal employee in the Treasury Department. There were two fellow clerks, white and very elderly, occupying with me the same room, with my door between theirs. One of them was a one-armed veteran of the Civil War and a Native of New England, inherited all traditions. The other was an intense partisan of the South, untouched in spirit by the influence which overcame slavery, but yet a man of unusual culture. It is amusing to recall how any question about the Civil War, innocently enough asked by me would bring them into verbal conflict. They were both to me warm personal friends such as I hope never to forget in time or eternity. It was the Southerner, Mr. Thomas H. Gibbs, who knew a little about the Bahá'í Teachings and was most urgent and insistent that I attend a meeting, which I had no inclination to do: as although I had been seeking, but not finding truth, had given up, because he had exacted a promise, and I thought to do him a favor. I went one cold, blustery, extremely unpleasant night to the address he gave me. . .[1]

Louis Gregory, one of the most consequential teachers of the Bahá'í Faith in the U.S., first heard of the Faith from an elderly supporter of the Confederate cause. Not only did Thomas Gibbs mention the Faith first to Gregory, but he also "insisted" that a reluctant Gregory learn more about it. Thus, Gibbs became the "means of guiding me to the spiritual forces which for many years have directed my life."[2]

On that stormy night of late 1907, Gregory entered the room in the Corona building across from his work where Pauline Hannen greeted him warmly and gave him a copy of *The Hidden Words, Daily Book,*[3] and a short essay written by Charles Mason Remey, one of the most knowledgeable Bahá'ís in the country at that time. Millie York and Nellie Gray, among the first Black American women to become Bahá'ís in D.C., joined them, and they all listened to Lua Getsinger give a short talk.

Born in upstate New York, Getsinger was raised on the millennial zeal of her mother. The people of that region were known for their belief that Jesus was coming soon. They were on fire with this hope, so much so that this part of the country came to be known as the "burned-over district." She studied drama in Chicago where she joined the Order of the Magi, a Masonic Lodge that taught that the Spirit of Christ was alive on earth. She first heard of the Bahá'í Faith at the World's Parliament of Religions in 1893 and, while studying with Dr. Kheiralla, came to understand that Bahá'u'lláh was the returned Christ. Soon she was introducing the Faith to her family members who then became Bahá'ís. She traveled around the country spreading the new message and, after hearing her, Mrs. Phoebe Hearst and Mr. Robert Turner accepted the Faith. These two were later known respectively as "Mother of the Faithful" and a "Disciple of 'Abdu'l-Bahá."[4]

At the meeting in the Corcoran building, Getsinger gave a historical account of the lives of the Báb and Bahá'u'lláh and the suffering of the early Bahá'ís that moved Gregory who described it as "vivid."[5] At the end of the evening, Pauline Hannen invited him to another meeting.

Interested in what he heard and in Mrs. Hannen's enthusi-asm, Louis Gregory attended this second meeting which was at the home of Carrie York and her mother, Millie York—"among poor people"—as he described the home. Pauline Hannen came and spoke about the Faith. Gregory was impressed by her "loving service."[6] They read passages from the Bahá'í Holy Writings. Pauline Hannen remembers Gregory being so taken with "the Words of Bahá'u'lláh as revealed in 'the Iqan' that he could not let go."[7] The "Iqan," or "Book of Certitude," is the second most important Book in the Scriptures of the Bahá'í Faith. One of its themes is the continuous unfoldment of God's Religion which is demonstrated in the Iqan using passages from the Bible and the Qur'an. The Bahá'í Writings, Gregory remembered, gave him an "entirely new conception of Christianity."[8]

The Hannens invited Gregory to their home to continue to learn about the Faith which he did for the next year and a half: "Mr. Hannen thus became my teacher, a service in which he was aided by his wife." For Pauline Hannen, Gregory was an answer to her personal prayer in their work of trying to reach Black Americans with the new Message: "We had been praying that someone among the Negro Race would arise to serve them more effectively. We believed Louis to be the answer."[9]

Louis Gregory's interest in the Bahá'í Faith opened the door to reaching educated Black Americans with the Bahá'í Message. His rise to professional prominence and his spiritual discernment are tributes to the people from whom he came and his own perseverance in the face of great odds.

Gregory's maternal grandmother was born into slavery.[10] His maternal grandfather, George Washington Dargan, was a planter and slave owner in South Carolina. In an extraordinarily charitable passage, Gregory remembers the Dargans this way:

> . . . outstanding and distinguished for their work in the field of religion and education. They accepted the end of slavery cheerfully and stimulated progress and enlightenment of humanity. I did not choose them as my forebearers, but in justice must acknowledge my obligations to them.[11]

Gregory was born on June 6, 1874,[12] towards the end of the Reconstruction period which saw federal troops and organizations in the Southern States working to prepare for the integration of Black Americans into the economic and political life of the region. Many gains were made but by 1876, the political resolve to maintain this effort weakened. In a backroom deal to elect Rutherford B. Hayes as President, the Reconstruction efforts ended with the promise from the Southern States that they would protect the rights of Black Americans. Once the troops left, these States enacted law after law to prevent the economic and political advancement of the new citizens, and to curb the rights they were supposed to share with their fellow white citizens. The Ku Klux Klan was founded during the Reconstruction to prevent any advance of Black Americans and others into the public arena by using physical intimidation and lethal violence. The Klan murdered the man Gregory's maternal grandmother married after emancipation.[13]

Faced with virtually insurmountable odds, newly freed Black Americans banded together in their families, free towns, and churches, to aid and uplift one another, founded schools and businesses, develop music and art, and pursue legal grievances when possible. They created spaces of success for themselves even though they were publicly enclosed in a wall of white racism.

Louis Gregory came from a family that found a way forward. His mother, Mary Elizabeth, and his stepfather, George Gregory,[14] were raised to be courteous, literate, and disciplined, with religious beliefs which "involved the mystery of a change of heart and putting of ideals into action."[15] He distinguished himself by earning a bachelor's degree from the Tuskegee Institute and a law degree from Howard University in a time when less than one percent of Black Americans had the opportunity to get an advanced education.[16] As noted above, Gregory met Thomas Gibbs as co-workers at the Treasury Department. Gibbs, a white Southerner, encouraged him to look into the Bahá'í Faith. That Gregory would be able to befriend and follow the advice of someone of this background spoke

Agnes Parsons, asked to organize a Race Amity Conference in Washington D.C. by 'Abdu'l-Baha in 1920.

to his courage and broad-mindedness. This same courage would allow him to bring the Message to educated Black Americans and endure the ridicule of professing such bold and new beliefs.

The Bahá'í teachings also greatly challenged Agnes Parsons, a wealthy white socialite, and took her on a journey beyond the assumptions of her upbringing, a journey she had the openness and courage to make. Born into privilege, she had no reason to question the values of the social circles of the upper class, white Washingtonians through which her parents, General and Mrs. Royal, and she moved. By 1908, she was middle-aged and settled into family life with her husband Jeffrey Parsons, and their two children, Jeffrey and Royall. And yet, at around the same time as Louis Gregory, she too encountered the Bahá'í teachings.[17] They attracted her so much that she took the risk of opening her home in February of that year to a series of talks by Ali Kuli Khan who spoke about the Faith to her friends. She caught the spirit of the Faith but was not yet a confirmed believer. To make a final judgment about the Faith, she decided that she would have to make a pilgrimage to 'Abdu'l-Bahá.

On August 31, 1908, 'Abdu'l-Bahá was freed after forty years as a political prisoner. He had come to Akka with His Father and the Holy family as a young man of twenty-four and took his first steps of freedom as a sixty-four-year-old with grey hair. And yet, He had always been free:

> After being forty years a prisoner I can tell you that freedom is not a matter of place. It is a condition. Unless one accepts dire vicissitudes, he will not attain. When one is released from the prison of self, that is indeed a release.[18]

The first place He visited after his official release was the tomb of His Father, Bahá'u'lláh, at Bahji. As a boy, 'Abdu'l-Bahá accompanied his mother to the underground dungeon where Bahá'u'lláh had been held during the time of persecution in 1852:

> I saw a dark, steep place. We entered a small, narrow doorway, and went down two steps, but beyond those one could see nothing. In the middle of the stairway, all of a sudden we heard His [Bahá'u'lláh's] . . . voice: 'Do not bring him in here', and so they took me back.[19]

In that dungeon, Bahá'u'lláh had a vision of a Maid of Heaven from whom He received a Divine Revelation:

> Pointing with her finger unto My head, she addressed all who are in heaven and all who are on earth, saying: 'By God! This is the Best-Beloved of the worlds, and yet ye comprehend not. This is the Beauty of God amongst you, and the power of His sovereignty within you, could ye but understand. This is the Mystery of God and His Treasure, the Cause of God and His glory unto all who are in the kingdoms of Revelation and of creation, if ye be of them that perceive.'[20]

She guaranteed victory to this new Revelation sent from God:

> Verily, We shall render Thee victorious by Thyself and by Thy Pen. Grieve Thou not for that which hath befallen Thee, neither be Thou afraid, for Thou art in safety. Erelong will God raise up the treasures of the earth—men who will aid Thee through Thyself and through Thy Name, wherewith God hath revived the hearts of such as have recognized Him.[21]

Bahá'u'lláh and His family were sent into exile in the winter of 1853. Along the way, the young 'Abdu'l-Bahá developed a case of frostbite; He had already had tuberculosis a few years earlier, and would suffer recurrences of ill health.

After the exiles arrived in Baghdad, Bahá'u'lláh went into seclusion in the wilderness that would last for two years. During His Absence, 'Abdu'l-Bahá took up more of the managing of the affairs of the Holy Family, including hand copying the Writings of the Báb and Bahá'u'lláh for distribution.[22] In the mosques of Baghdad, the teenage 'Abdu'l-Bahá could be seen discussing the Qur'an. Upon His Father's Return, 'Abdu'l-Bahá fell to his knees in front of him, sobbing.[23]

Bahá'u'lláh, the Holy Family, and their companions were exiled again in 1863. Before their departure, in the Garden of Ridvan, Bahá'u'lláh revealed that He was the Manifestation of God, the Promised One of All Ages.

During the arduous journey to Constantinople, 'Abdu'l-Bahá helped to provide for all the exiles. Bahá'u'lláh described His eldest son as "... *this sacred and glorious Being, this Branch of Holiness.* .." and that "... *well is it with him that hath sought His shelter and abideth beneath His shadow.*"[24]

By the time 'Abdu'l-Bahá was in his twenties, He was managing the affairs of the Holy Family. On their arrival in Akka, Palestine, on their third exile in the sweltering summer of 1868, many of the exiles fell ill in the cramped prison quarters.[25] 'Abdu'l-Bahá sought medication and tended to the sick while he himself became ill with dysentery. He endured the painful loss of his younger brother who fell through a skylight.

In Akka, He took responsibility for the interactions between the exiles and the world beyond the prison. The local people and authorities came to have respect for these exiles, whom they had been told to shun, and developed a special affection for 'Abdu'l-Bahá.

Upon being finally freed from any form of restrictive confinement in 1908, 'Abdu'l-Bahá set his sights on guiding the followers of His Father who were now found in lands far away from the lands in which the Faith had been born.

For over ten years, 'Abdu'l-Bahá received and sent letters from the growing number of believers in the West. He encouraged them in the growth of their devotion, faithfulness, constancy, and, most of all, He urged them to work towards one goal: unity.

To a new Bahá'í in Washington, D.C., He wrote:

> . . . in the Kingdom of God all are the same, whether black or white. The greater the Faith of either, the more acceptable he is in the Kingdom. . . . God looks at hearts not upon colors. He looks upon qualities not upon bodies.[26]

Notes

1. Louis Gregory, quoted in Moe, *Aflame with Devotion*, 73.
2. Louis Gregory, quoted in Morrison, *To Move the World*, 75.
3. The authors are not sure what the *Daily Reader* was. According to the U.S. Bahá'í Archives: "Regrettably . . . we don't know of any daily reader dating from that early period. One of us thinks it's possible that Louis Gregory might be referring to Helen Goodall's 'Daily Lessons Received in Acca' which had been published in 1908, but that is only a supposition."
4. 'Abdu'l-Bahá gave Phoebe Hearst this title and said that her name would be uplifted and spread around in the future. Shoghi Effendi transformed the Mansion of Bahji into a museum that would display the achievements of the Bahá'í Faith. He placed the portrait of Phoebe Hearst in a room overlooking the Shrine of Bahá'u'lláh for her contributions to the growth of the Faith in the West. Robert Turner was named a "Disciple of Bahá'u'lláh" by Shoghi Effendi (authors' note).
5. Louis Gregory, quoted in Moe, *Aflame with Devotion*, 74.
6. Ibid., 74.
7. Ibid., 75
8. Louis Gregory, quoted in Morrison, *To Move the World*, xiii.
9. Louis Gregory, quoted in Moe, *Aflame with Devotion*, 75.
10. Morrison, *To Move the World*, 12.
11. Louis Gregory, quoted in ibid., 12.
12. Ibid., 8.
13. Ibid., 13.
14. Louis Gregory's birth father was Ebenezer (Morrison, "Gregory, Louis George").
15. Louis Gregory, quoted in Morrison, *To Move the World*, 12.
16. Statistical Abstract Supplement No. HS-2. Population Characteristics: 1900 to 2002 of the United States: 2003, Census. U.S. Census Bureau, 2003; "The College-bred Negro American."
17. Her primary teacher of the Faith was most likely Lua Getsinger who was in D.C. actively teaching, corresponded with her regularly during those years, and accompanied her on her pilgrimage in 1910 (authors' note).
18. Dodge, "'Abdu'l-Bahá's Arrival," *Star of the West*, 1912, 4.
19. Balyuzi, *'Abdu'l-Bahá*, 12.
20. Bahá'u'lláh, quoted in Shoghi Effendi, *God Passes By*, 101-102.
21. Bahá'u'lláh, *Epistle to the Son of the Wolf*, 21.
22. Balyuzi, *'Abdu'l-Bahá*, 14.
23. Ibid., 15.

24. Bahá'u'lláh, *The Tablet of the Branch*, quoted in Shoghi Effendi, *World Order*, 135.
25. Balyuzi cites the names of sixty-seven exiles accompanying Baha'u'llah into exile. H. M. Balyuzi, *Baha'u'llah*, p 28.
26. Tablet of 'Abdu'l-Bahá to Mrs. Marie Botay, sent through Mrs. Carrie Kinney, Acca, 1909, *Star of the West*, 1909, 108.

Louis Gregory, Howard University Law School Graduate, class of 1902

Chapter 5

Herald of the Kingdom

There could be no greater news for Christians than that Jesus had returned and the promises of the Bible were fulfilled. This Good News is what drew many of the early American Bahá'ís to the Faith.

They came into a new spiritual life in the Bahá'í community but had been shaped by the old traditions of the society in which they'd been raised. Most white Americans who became Bahá'ís had never questioned, for example, the assumptions they and their families and friends held about race and segregation.

To grow towards a truer imitation of the life of the Master, they had to allow His guidance and the Writings to change them. Gradually, day by day, they could then let go of old, long-accepted ideas and be transformed. Doing so would liberate them from the shackles of the past but it would also invite criticism, ridicule, and social rejection from the people in their present lives.

In the American society of the early 1900s, Jim Crow[1] was in its ascendency. Public spaces were racially segregated. The economic and social structures such as housing and job opportunities also followed this pattern. As a result, segregation affected the private sphere as well, and so, white and Black Americans did not associate much privately, if at all.

The popular culture reflected the racism of the segregation laws. When the Black American boxing champion, Jack Johnson, won a title fight in 1909 against a white boxer, a famous white writer fearfully proclaimed that ". . . the White Man must be rescued."[2] A country-wide search was undertaken to find some-one who could defeat Jack Johnson. When such a white fighter was found, James Jeffries, he was described as "The Great White Hope." When Johnson defeated Jeffries as well, rioting in cities throughout the nation ensued during which Black Americans were injured and murdered.[3]

A narrative of Black progress was also promoted to highlight gains made by Black Americans. In his inaugural address the new President, William Howard Taft, outlined this view:

The negroes are now Americans. Their ancestors came here years ago against their will, and this is their only country and their only flag. They have shown themselves anxious to live for it and to die for it. Encountering the race feeling against them, subjected at times to cruel injustice growing out of it, they may well have our profound sympathy and aid in the struggle they are making. We are charged with the sacred duty of making their path as smooth and easy as we can. Any recognition of their distinguished men, any appointment to office from among their number, is properly taken as an en-couragement and an appreciation of their progress, and this just policy should be pursued when suitable occasion offers.[4]

Booker T. Washington exemplified most famously the strenu-ous efforts of Black Americans to work for their own economic progress in the face of segregation and disenfranchisement. He stressed the central role of education and business development and working with the available institutions and like-minded white philanthropists as ways to uplift Black Americans econom-ically. Other Black American leaders wanted to focus more on gaining political power to advance economic progress for Black Americans. One outcome of this view was the founding in 1909 of the National Association for the Advancement of Colored People. After the race riots in 1908 in Springfield, Illinois, in which seven Black residents were murdered, a group of white Americans called for a meeting to address the situation and the underlying causes and Black leaders, including W. E. B. Du Bois, Ida B. Wells-Barnett, and Mary Church Terrell, joined them. The NAACP was formed with this mission:

> To promote equality of rights and eradicate caste or race prejudice among citizens of the United States; to advance the interest of colored citizens; to secure for them impartial suffrage; and to increase their opportunities for securing justice in the courts, education for their children, employment according to their ability, and complete equality before the law.[5]

The same month as the NAACP was founded in New York City, Joseph Hannen wrote—based on instructions from 'Abdu'l-Bahá—that ". . . to prove the validity of our Teachings and as a means of removing existing prejudices between the races, a Spiritual Assembly or meeting be held, preferably at the home of one of the white Bahá'ís, in which both races should join."[6]

In June of that year, 1909, Louis Gregory became a "confirmed believer."[7] He had studied the Bahá'í Faith for over a year with the Hannens.

In the early part of the year, the couple made a pilgrimage to 'Abdu'l-Bahá in the Holy Land, during which time Gregory lost contact with Bahá'ís and focused on the establishment of his legal practice on 1553 4th St., NW. Later, he learned that while the Hannens were on pilgrimage:

> . . . they had kindly mentioned me to the Master who had instructed them to continue teaching me, assuring them that I would become a believer and an advocate of the teachings. Upon their return they remade the connection. Through the very unusual kindness of these dear friends, my mental

veils were cleared away and the light of assurance mercifully appeared within when they had taught me . . . how to pray.[8]

While the Hannens were on pilgrimage, 'Abdu'l-Bahá spoke to them of teaching Black Americans about the Faith. Pauline Hannen remembers about this important mission that she was "the first to work among them, and then later my sister, Alma Knobloch, and Joseph, my husband. Alma had gone to Germany so her work ceased with the colored people in Washington, but Joey and I continued without her." She hoped that:

> 'Abdu'l-Bahá would understand my work among the colored race, because I had many drawbacks. There were many to tell me I was wasting my time, that I would do much better and more credible work among my own people. When the boys of the neighborhood knew that colored people were coming to meetings at our house, they would throw bricks and stones and overripe tomatoes and vegetables in our vestibule, and also unhinge the front gate. I would sit by the door in the hall and quietly hide these things back of the vestibule door so that the friends never knew. My husband would unhinge the front gate and put it in a place of safety until the meeting was over, replacing it later. All these happenings really brought joy to my heart, and I believed, contrary to the others, that 'Abdu'l-Bahá would understand it all when I saw Him.[9]

One morning, 'Abdu'l-Bahá inquired about the relationship between the races in Washington, D.C. He said to Joseph Hannen, "May you be the means of uniting the colored and the white races. . ."[10] The Hannens carried on their teaching efforts by defying convention and inviting Black Americans to their home. 'Abdu'l-Bahá encouraged Joseph:

> Ye have written that the colored Bahá'ís have gathered in one meeting with the white Believers, destroying the foundation

of racial differences and the barriers of color. When a gathering of these two races is brought about, that assemblage will become the magnet of the Supreme Concourse and the Confirmations of the Blessed Perfection will surround it.[11]

Soon after their return, Gregory declared that he was a Bahá'í: "At length, as the lesson of humility took effect and every hope vanished save the Will of God, 'Abdu'l-Bahá . . . revealed himself."[12]

Gregory expressed his gratitude to the Hannens for teaching him the Faith:

It comes to me that I have never taken occasion to thank you specifically for all your kindness and patience, which finally culminated in my acceptance of the great truths of the Bahá'í Revelation. It has given me an entirely new conception of Christianity and of all religions, and with it my whole nature seems changed for the better . . . It is a sane and practical religion, which meets all the varying needs of life, and I hope I shall ever regard it as a priceless possession.[13]

Taking this great leap of faith was a very risky one for Gregory. Many of his friends and colleagues were astonished and expressed criticism bordering on ridicule:

By far the majority of my friends thought I had become mentally unbalanced. One of my old teachers, a professor of international law and a very affectionate friend, almost wept over my departure from orthodoxy and with others warned me that I was blasting all hopes of a career. The *Washington Bee*, a well-known colored newspaper, on one occasion gave me two columns of ridicule which remained unanswered. Others, knowing my controversial habits (i.e., habit of engaging in controversy) of the past said, "He must have religion since he does not answer that!"[14]

This article in the *Washington Bee* contained outright mockery of Gregory and the Faith. One person is quoted as saying that "I had a talk with Louis Gregory recently and he sprung that Baha substitute for orthodox religion on me." Gregory had become "tangled up with dope that is musty with age" and was now a "minor leaguer Baha" but that someday "he will forget that Baha ever wore a Turban."[15]

His friends also pointed out that the Bahá'í community in D.C. followed the patterns of segregation of the broader society:

> As soon as I became a believer and began to teach, however, my colored friends got on my back and began to press me with troublous questions. If this were a New religion which stood for unity, why were its devotees divided? Why did they not meet in one place? Were the Bahá'ís not full of prejudice like other people?[16]

Gregory realized that he would have an important role in helping the Bahá'ís of D.C. with this issue. His extraordinary combination of forthrightness, courage, and humble sense of service comes through in this note to the Hannens as well as his understanding of the greatness of the "Cause" and, therefore, the need to protect it:

> If you are not busy Saturday evening, I want to have a talk with you and have a clear understanding in regard to the attitude of the local assembly toward the colored believers. It is with sincere regret that I find it necessary to bring this matter up, and only because some impressions are going abroad which I fear will injure our Cause both among white and colored.
>
> I have nothing to complain of that is of a personal nature. But 'Abdu'l-Bahá has said that slight differences now may be great differences hereafter. And for this reason, I do not wish the awful responsibility of being the cause or occasion of any schism to rest upon my shoulders.[17]

Library of Congress

Library of Congress

Top left, Alain Locke
Top right, W. E. B. DuBois
Center, Langston Hughes
Bottom, Booker T. Washington

National Museum of American History

The Fourth Annual Conference of the National Association for the Advancement of Colored People at Chicago. Note Joseph Hannen is standing to the left of the open window where the children are sitting, standing beside W. E. B. DuBois.

By this time, Gregory's prominence in D.C.'s Black society rose, making his declaration as a Bahá'í even riskier. He was chosen as the new President of the Bethel Literary and Historical Society a month after his declaration. The *Washington Bee* noted that Gregory was "bringing his society back to its former popularity."[18] Founded in 1881 by Bishop Daniel A. Payne of the African Methodist Church,[19] the Society ". . . captured the imagination of highly literate middle- and upper-class Black Americans who struggled to find new strategies to promote racial advancement and develop self-confidence . . ."[20] and remained active until 1915. Black Americans from all around D.C. were invited to attend the regularly scheduled events which were welcoming to new people—the mailings encouraged people to bring their friends. This openness set the Bethel Society apart from other literary societies which required participants to have certain social credentials.[21]

Gregory wrote to Joseph Hannen that he wanted to use his new position as President of the Bethel Society to hold a large meeting at the Bethel Society and introduce the Bahá'í teachings and that he hoped this would turn into a series.[22] Being head of the Society gave Gregory the unique opportunity to introduce the Bahá'í Faith to educated Black Americans of Washington, D.C., and he seized that opportunity. As a result of his efforts, leading Black scholars and intellectuals such as Booker T. Washington, Langston Hughes, W. E. B. Dubois, and Alain Locke would hear of the Bahá'í teachings for the first time.

After he became a Bahá'í in June, Gregory wrote to 'Abdu'l-Bahá declaring his belief as was the custom for Bahá'ís to do in those days, and in November, he received this reply from 'Abdu'l-Bahá charging him with a great mission:

> HE IS GOD! O, thou wooer of Truth! Thy letter was received. Its contents indicated thy attainment to the Most Great Guidance. Thank thou God that thou hast attained to such a Bounty, discovered the Path of the Kingdom and received the Glad Tidings of the Universe of the Most High. This Divine Bestowal is conducive to the everlasting Glory in both worlds. I hope that thou mayest become the herald of the Kingdom; become the means whereby the white and colored people shall close their eyes to racial differences and behold the reality of humanity: And that is the universal unity which is the oneness of the kingdom of the human race, the basic harmony of the world and the appearance of the Bounty of the Almighty. In brief, do thou not look upon thy weak body and thy limited capacity. Look thou upon the Bounties and Providence of the Lord of the Kingdom; for His Confirmation is great and His Power unparalleled and incomparable. Rely as much as thou canst upon the True One and be thou resigned to the Will of God, so that like unto a candle thou mayest become enkindled in the world of humanity and like unto a star thou mayest shine and gleam from the Horizon of Reality and become the cause of the Guidance of both races. Upon thee be Baha el Abha![23]

This message from 'Abdu'l-Bahá may well have been a turning point for Gregory. He left his law practice and decided to devote himself full-time to the spreading of the new Message. He now became the "herald of the Kingdom" and an instrument through which the Black and the white could be united by the Divine Spirit.

Notes

1. The 'Jim Crow' laws refer to laws found all over the United States requiring racial segregation in all public spaces.
2. Frank Sennett, "Hall of Hate."
3. Gustkey, "80 Years Ago."
4. Taft, "Inaugural Address of William Howard Taft."
5. Snowden-McCray, "The NAACP Was Established February 12, 1909."
6. Joseph Hannen, "Washington, D.C.," 18-19.
7. Louis Gregory, quoted in Morrison, *To Move the World*, 5.
8. Louis Gregory, quoted in ibid, 5.
9. Pauline Hannen, quoted in Moe, *Aflame with Devotion*, , 136.
10. Pauline Hannen, quoted in ibid., 136.
11. 'Abdu'l-Bahá, Tablet to Joseph Hannen, through Mirza Moneer Zain (No date given on letter), starts "Thy letter dated July 12th . . .", Translation of 'Abdu'l-Bahá Collection, US Bahá'í National Archives, quoted in Moe, *Aflame with Devotion*, 141.
12. Louis Gregory, quoted in Morrison, *To Move the World*, 5.
13. Louis Gregory, quoted in Moe, *Aflame with Devotion*, 75.
14. Louis Gregory, quoted in Morrison, *To Move the World*, 30.
15. The Sage of the Potomac, "Public Men and Things."
16. Louis Gregory, quoted in Morrison, *To Move the World*, 5.
17. Louis Gregory, quoted in ibid., 6.
18. "The Week in Society," *The Washington Bee*, 06 Nov., 1909, 5.
19. A Protestant denomination founded by Black Americans that advocated strenuously for civil rights. While housed in the church, the society sought to remain independent of it (McHenry, *Recovering the Lost History*, 152).
20. Ibid., 182.
21. Ibid., 152.

22. Morrison, *To Move the World*, 32-33.

23. Tablet from 'Abdu'l-Bahá to Louis Gregory, translated by Mirza Ahmad Sohrab, Nov. 17, 1909, historical document, quoted in Gregory, *A Heavenly Vista*.

Chapter 6

The Race Question

Aherald is an 'official messenger bringing news.' In 1910, Gregory became just such an official messenger. The news he was bringing in this case was the news of the "Kingdom"— there was a new Divine Revelation sent to bring about the unity of the human race. He was "official" because he was acting on the expressed hope of 'Abdu'l-Bahá through whom the power and authority of this Revelation flowed.

Gregory set forth on a speaking tour of the South in the early part of that year. He travelled through Richmond, Virginia; Durham, North Carolina; Charleston, South Carolina; and Macon, Georgia, among other places. His letters back conveyed enthusiasm because ". . . in every city people were found who accepted the great Message, however crudely and abruptly given, and the spirit was powerful. . .", and he felt that Black Americans in the South seemed to be "deeply and vitally interested."[1]

The Master's spiritual power flowed through Gregory when giving the Message. He was a channel. He remembers a dream he had prior to his departure for a future speaking tour:

> . . . 'Abdu'l-Bahá was standing before an audience in the attitude of teaching. By his direction I was serving as a waiter, passing to the people bread from a tray. When the wafers reached the people, they were transformed into tablets and upon them they were to indicate how many of them accepted the teachings and became Bahá'ís. An overwhelming number

of those who received the tablets thus signified by writing their acceptance. I awoke feeling very happy.

By the way, the doors are opened to deliver the Message and the happiness manifested among those who give ear, this dream becomes a glorious reality.[2]

Louis Gregory's spirit was soaring but the new world he perceived with his faith had not yet dawned.

Throughout 1910, meetings for the teaching of the Bahá'í Faith and bringing together Black and white people in a spirit of unity gathered momentum.

On March 6, 1910, the Hannens opened their home for a meeting to teach about the Bahá'í Faith to which twelve Black Americans came and thirty-five guests in all.[3] The Hannens were continuing their efforts—encouraged by 'Abdu'l-Bahá in His letter to Joseph a year earlier to invite Black Americans to his home to demonstrate the Bahá'í teachings of unity among the races in concrete action and for the white Bahá'ís to take that initiative:

> In February of last year, 'Abdu'l-Bahá commanded that to prove the validity of our Teachings and as a means of removing existing prejudices between the races, a Spiritual Assembly or meeting be held, preferably at the home of one of the white Bahá'ís, in which both races could join.[4]

They may also have been awakened to this need by Louis Gregory who wrote to the Working Committee for the Bahá'ís of D.C. about the segregation in the community that reflected the values of the society but not of the Bahá'í teachings.[5]

In reporting on this meeting, Hannen also noted that "a regular meeting is being held at the home of Mr. and Mrs. Dyer, 1937 13th St. N.W. on Wednesdays."[6] Gregory taught this couple the Faith. Maggie Dyer was born into slavery of African and Irish ancestry. Growing up to be active in charitable causes, she funded the Ladies' Unity Benevolent Society of the District of Columbia in 1909.[7] Andrew Dyer was born into slavery and was of African and French descent. He worked as a messenger in a department of the government. Their home became a center for gatherings of inter-racial spiritual fellowship. At one of their Wednesday meetings on June 15, 1910, the first French Bahá'í, Hippolyte Dreyfuss, spoke to a large audience of both Black and white people.[8]

Among those attending the Wednesday meetings at the Dyers was Coralie Franklin Cook. Her parents, Albert Barbour Franklin and Mary Elizabeth Edmondson, were born into slavery in Virginia. They were descendants of Elizabeth Hemmings of the Hemmings family whose members, though enslaved, occupied important positions on Thomas Jefferson's estate, Monticello. The Franklins were an aristocratic and educated family with whom Cook had close daily interactions. After emancipation, her father became a highly respected member of his community and placed his two daughters in the Storer Normal School at Harpers Ferry, West Virginia, the only school of higher education for Black Americans in the state. A gifted student, Cook continued her education in Boston and Philadelphia. She moved to Washington, D.C. where she became Head of the Colored Home for Orphans and Aged Women. She married George Cook, a professor at Howard University, where she became the Chair of Oratory. A powerful presence and speaker, she was active in the women's movement including in the struggle for the right to vote—Cook "exemplified the third generation of African American women suffragists who related to both the Black and the white worlds."[9]

Cook learned of the Faith at the meetings in the Dyer residence in 1910, and formally became a Bahá'í in 1913. In writing to Joseph Hannen about her attraction to the Bahá'í Faith, she noted that her friends, ". . . were very generally impressed not only with the wisdom of your teaching but with the earnestness and *sincerity* of the teachers."[10] During those years, she introduced the Faith to many Black intellectuals and students at Howard University. She thought the teachings could uplift Black Americans.[11] She organized regular meetings on campus. At one of these, Roy Wilhelm, a white Bahá'í, spoke and "... though the rain continued, a number of most interested souls, leaders among the colored race, listened attentively to the glad-tidings."[12]

Cook wrote to Pauline Hannen about a recent Bahá'í speaker who spoke to an audience of Black American women:

> Mr. Cook tells me that you and Mr. H. heard Mr. Madden last Sunday. Is he not a man of splendid courage and a true servant of the Blessed Perfection [Bahá'u'lláh]"? I wish many more could have seen that audience and witnessed the promise in our girls for the future womanhood of the race. It was altogether fitting that a group of *young* women should conceive and carry out the idea of bringing him before a group of those he had recently so defended and protected.[13]

Gregory also increased his efforts to teach the Faith to educated Black Americans through public meetings at the Bethel Literary and Cultural Association; there were four well-attended meetings. Joseph Hannen reported in *Bahá'í News*, the new Bahá'í national journal:

> The Bethel Literary and Historical Society, the oldest and leading colored organization in the city, devoted its session of Tuesday, April 5, 1910, to the Bahá'í Revelation, Mr. Hannen and Dr. Fareed speaking on the subject of "The Race Question from the Standpoint of the Bahá'í Revelation." This Society, of which Mr. Louis G. Gregory is President, has given three previous sessions this season to the Bahá'í Teachings, and this has exerted a powerful influence in the work among the intelligent circles of this people, whom we are commanded to reach and help as brothers and sisters.[14]

The Bahá'ís of D.C. organized regular "Unity Feasts" which were the forerunners of the Nineteen-Day Feasts at which Bahá'ís would gather for devotions, community consultation, and fellowship. Despite their name, the Unity Feasts had still been segregated, as was the custom of the country. It was decided to change this and that every fourth feast would be "held in such a manner that both races can join."[15] Louis Gregory spoke at the first of the integrated feasts on April 9, 1910, while Fanny Knobloch served as hostess. This feast was held in the home of Mr. H. S. Cragin, a lawyer, and his aunt, the widowed Martha F. Stamper, who worked as a clerk. The house had a large double parlor, allowing more people to attend.[16]

Joseph Hannen described this gathering as "wonderfully blessed and successful" and noted that "several leading men and women of the colored race attended." Most of all it was a "radical step in this section of the country and is in reality making history."[17]

To accommodate more participants in the Unity Feasts, the space at the Washington Conservatory of Music at 902 T St. NW was donated by Mrs. Harriet Gibbs Marshall, the President of the Conservatory, an organization she founded in 1903. Coralie Cook and Louis Gregory were involved with this school and must have made the contact.

Marshall was the daughter of Mifflin Wistar Gibbs, the first Black American city judge in the U.S., and Maria Ann Alexander, a schoolteacher. She was born in Canada because her father had fled California after he and others were forced to wear race badges.[18] Marshall went on to become a distinguished and dedicated music educator. She became a Bahá'í in the 1910s. When her husband, a military officer, was appointed to a position in Haiti, she was able to introduce the Bahá'í Faith there.[19]

During the 1910s, the Bahá'í Faith was proclaimed and taught to numerous Black Americans, especially among the educated. Within the Bahá'í community, there was a growing acceptance of the importance of holding interracial gatherings as being the truest reflection of the Bahá'í teachings on the oneness of humankind. The segregationist laws and customs of the country, though, were stronger than ever—in the workplace, in the social spaces, and in the private sphere of the home—and had a continued impact on the Bahá'í community despite the undoubted sincerity of the Bahá'ís.

Many gatherings—the Friday meetings at 1219 Connecticut Ave, NW, the Sunday school, the classes on Bible prophecies and the Bahá'í Writings—may still have been segregated. Though these gatherings, Joseph Hannen noted, had "proven to be most helpful in the spread of the Teachings, through the spirit of love and unity which is noticeable there and attracts the seekers as seemingly nothing else can. . .", he also singles out the March 6th meeting as "representing the joining in one meeting of the white and the colored Bahá'ís and friends of this city. . ."[20] implying that the two races did not mingle in the other gatherings.

This was Louis Gregory's insightful analysis in hindsight of the situation:

> One matter that caused much difficulty in adjustment was the wise handling of the American race problem, especially in the Southern atmosphere of such a city as Washington. Some of the friends, reading the command of Bahá'u'lláh which read: "Close your eyes to racial differences and welcome all with the light of oneness," interpreted it to mean that all barriers of race should be put aside in every meeting that was planned for teaching the Faith. Others knew the principle as wise and just, but felt that the time was not yet ripe for its application. One difficulty was finding places, either private or public, that were willing to welcome all races. In the same family, one or more members being Bahá'í and the others not believers, the mixing of races would cause a family disturbance. Even where all the believers were free from prejudices some felt that it would upset inquirers after the truth if they were confronted too soon with signs of racial equality.[21]

In 1908, the Young Turk movement forced constitutional changes in the Ottoman Empire which included the release of many political prisoners. Suddenly, 'Abdu'l-Bahá was free for the first time in well over half a century. He had entered Akka as a prisoner at age twenty-four and was freed at the age of sixty-four.

The first act He did as a free person was to visit His Father's shrine at Bahji near Akka. His great desire now was to develop a garden next to the shrine to beautify the area. He carried jars from the well as many as sixty times a week to water the new garden. Despite his advanced age and the physical ailments brought on by years of tests and difficulties, this act of devotion brought him great joy.[22]

The Bahá'í Faith, of which 'Abdu'l-Bahá was the divinely-inspired head, was well established in parts of Central Asia and Iran. He set his sights now on broader horizons. He decided to go west to Europe and North America and water the gardens of the hearts of the Bahá'ís so that they and their small Bahá'í communities could grow and develop. His journey began with a trip to Egypt in 1910.

Agnes Parsons had been interested in the Bahá'í Faith for several years but had not become a Bahá'í herself. The new Faith and its teachings were foreign to the Washington social circles through which she and her husband moved.

She decided she would seek certainty about the truth of the Bahá'í Faith by making a pilgrimage to 'Abdu'l-Bahá in 1910. Approaching the Bay of Haifa, she felt both "curiosity and hope."[23] She would essentially be judging the divine origins of the Faith by the person of 'Abdu'l-Bahá.

'Abdu'l-Bahá was tending to other business when Parsons arrived for her appointment with him at his house on Haparsim Street in Haifa so she had to wait. She felt some irritation as she was used to promptness in her tightly scheduled life. When she finally did enter his presence, "a ray of blinding light seemed to pass from His eyes to hers."[24] She collapsed at his feet. As she came to, she realized that 'Abdu'l-Bahá was helping her to stand back up.

While visiting the Tomb of Bahá'u'lláh the next day, she saw that the flowers were swaying back and forth despite there being no breeze. A small bird flew to her and came to rest in her dress, near her heart.[25]

These and other incidents which she experienced as mystical

signs and pregnant with meaning for her spiritual search, confirmed her faith. In meeting 'Abdu'l-Bahá, she found what she was
looking for.

Bahá'ís in the West were cherishing the hope that the Master
would come to their countries and teach them. Agnes Parsons
wrote:

> When in 1910 I went to Haifa on my first visit to 'Abdu'l-Bahá,
> there were rumors that He might come to America now that
> the way was open for Him to travel. Many of the friends whom
> I met said they could not picture 'Abdu'l-Bahá in a western
> setting, but from the moment I heard the subject mentioned
> I thought He would come. One day when He was giving me
> instruction I said: "When you come to America will you stay
> with us?" He smiled at my confident "when" and answered:
> "Yes,"[26]

Notes

1. Louis Gregory, quoted in Morrison, *To Move the World*, 35.
2. Louis Gregory in a letter to a friend in Tulsa, OK, Nov. 25, 1916, *Star of the West*.
3. This has been described as the first formal interracial Bahá'í gathering (Moe, 77). This may be because the Working Committee organized them, though this is speculation. The authors have not used this characterization here as the Hannens had been meeting with Black American seekers for some time already.
4. *Bahá'í News*, v. 1, n. 1, quoted in Morrison, *To Move the World*, 33.
5. Stockman, *The Bahá'í Faith*, vol. 2, 344.
6. *Bahá'í News*, v. 1, n. 1, quoted in Morrison, *To Move the World*, 33. Race is a constructed reality not a biological or spiritual one. About the race of Dyers, Dr. Christopher Buck writes: "In those days, race constituted a social identity marker and the basis for pervasive social discrimination. One of the early American Bahá'ís, Andrew Jackson Dyer, said to be African American, or of a "mixed" race, was born in 1847 in Virginia, and died in 1918 in Washington, D.C. Dyer was employed as a messenger in a government department. His wife, Maggie Jordan Dyer, became a Bahá'í in 1909. Born in March 1858 (also in Virginia) and married around 1876, Maggie J. Dyer was listed as "mulatto" in the 1880 and 1910 United States Census and, yet was listed as "white" in the 1900 United States Census." (Buck, Kolins, "African American Bahá'ís").
7. "Benevolent Society Incorporated."
8. Morrison, *To Move the World*, 33.
9. "Coralie Franklin Cook," 63.
10. Coralie Cook quoted in Etter-Lewis, Thomas, *Lights*, 72.
11. Etter-Lewis, Thomas, *Lights*, 71.
12. Hannen, "Washington, D.C.," *Bahá'í News*, v. 1, n. 3, April 28, 18-19.
13. Coralie Cook letter to Pauline Hannen, quoted in Etter-Lewis, Thomas, *Lights*, 72.
14. Hannen, "Washington, D.C.," *Bahá'í News*, v. 1, n. 2.
15. *Bahá'í News*, v. 1, n. 1, quoted in Morrison, *To Move the World*, 33.
16. Hannen, "Washington, D.C.," *Bahá'í News*, 19.
17. *Bahá'í News*, v. 1, n. 1, quoted in Morrison, *To Move the World*, 33.
18. "Notable Kentucy African Americans – Marshall, Harriet (Hattie) A. Gibbs."
19. Letter from Louis Gregory to Harriet Gibbs Marshall, in Darlene Clark Hine, *Black Women*, 54.
20. Hannen, "Washington D.C.," *Bahá'í News*, v. 1, n. 1, 18.
21. Louis Gregory, quoted in Morrison, *To Move the* World, 34.
22. Balyuzi, *'Abdu'l-Bahá*, 131.

23. Agnes Parson pilgrim's notes in a conversation recorded in McKay, "Devoted Handmaiden," 8. 'Pilgrim's notes' refers to the individual accounts of encounters with 'Abdu'l-Baha and should be taken as personal memories and not authenticated versions of the Master's words or actions.
24. Ibid., 8.
25. Ibid., 8.
26. Agnes Parson pilgrim's notes, U.S. Bahá'í National Archives.

A Heavenly Vista

"AND I JOHN SAW
THE HOLY CITY,
NEW JERUSALEM,
COMING DOWN FROM
GOD OUT OF
HEAVEN, PREPARED
AS A BRIDE
ADORNED FOR HER
HUSBAND"—REV. 21:2

THE PILGRIMAGE

OF

LOUIS G. GREGORY

Louis Gregory's book *A Heavenly Vista* detailng his pilgramage
to Egypt and the Holy Land.

Chapter 7

"Speak to Me, Mr. Gregory"

'Abdu'l-Bahá, the Servant of God and the Center of the Covenant of God, was found to be a loving father, a mighty teacher, and the living Temple in Whom the Spirit of Love abides. With the Manna of this Perfect Love He feeds the hearts of men. To discover His reality is to know this to a certainty. Today, in a world darkened by selfishness and sin, He walks unknown. Tomorrow, when the veils are rent, all men will want to know what He said and did. And the question will often be asked: "Is it possible that He even came amongst us and we knew Him not?"[1]

With these words, Louis Gregory begins the memoir of his life-changing pilgrimage to 'Abdu'l-Bahá and the Bahá'í Holy Places. After receiving permission from 'Abdu'l-Bahá in late 1910 to come on pilgrimage in the spring, he booked passage on a ship that included extra time on the return trip to travel to Europe and visit the Bahá'í communities there.

In February, during the months before his departure for Egypt, he was elected to the Working Committee for the Bahá'ís of D.C., the first step in what would become a distinguished life of service over many years on Bahá'í administrative bodies. He saw his election to the Committee as a sign of the racial progress of the Bahá'í community in D.C. He wrote to Joseph Hannen:

> I have your kind favor of the 4th, advising me of the action of the Working Committee of the Bahá'í Assembly in electing me to

membership. My emotion upon reading it was a commingling
of pleasure and [embarrassment]. There is joy because I know
that this action springs from a noble impulse on the part of the
committee. It evinces breadth and the Guidance of the Spirit.
Who knows how far-reaching the effect will be in advancing
the cause of God in the future?

The [embarrassment] is due to the fact that what is truly a
great honor should be given one so unworthy. I agree to serve
temporarily, until someone with a wise head and noble heart
may be found, who may thus more fitly represent my race.[2]

At the March meeting in their home, the Dyers hosted a surprise
going away party for Gregory to which more than fifty guests
came. After all, not only was this a major voyage under normal
circumstances, but this was also the first time a Black American
Bahá'í had been invited to come on pilgrimage to see 'Abdu'l-
Bahá. A proper send-off was necessary.[3] Gregory was seated at the
head of a long table, and his chair was surrounded by flowers from
the many well-wishers. Speeches were made by the distinguished
guests including Dr. W. B. Evans, Principal of the Armstrong
Manual Training School; Judge Gibbs, former U.S. Consul
to Madagascar; Professor G. W. Cook, of Harvard University;
Edward G. Braithwaite; Mr. Duffield; Ms. Murrell, a teacher at
the Armstrong Manual Training School; Ms. Grace Robarts; Mrs.
Claudia S. Coles; Mason Remey; Dr. Stanwood Cobb; and Joseph
and Pauline Hannen.

Gregory boarded the ship on March 25, 1911. Crossing the
Atlantic, he reflected on the forced journey made the other way
by his ancestors whose every human tie had been ruptured by
enslavement, and now here he was going back the other way, a
free man. Black Americans had made the ultimate sacrifices for
the U.S. and had adapted to a hostile environment to forge a place
of their own. Gregory concluded that "in fact no other American
group . . . is more American."[4]

He landed in Alexandria, Egypt, on the afternoon of April
10th. He made his way to the store owned by a Bahá'í, where

several Bahá'ís welcomed him. He had a letter of introduction from Edward Getsinger. The store owner asked him if he was prepared to see their lord. Gregory didn't want to take him away from his business but the owner brushed aside this concern saying that this was "spiritual business." Soon, they came to a modest house. They walked into the front garden and up to the second-story entrance where Gregory was soon ushered into the Master's presence.

Gregory describes 'Abdu'l-Bahá's appearance:

> 'Abdu'l-Bahá appeared about medium height, with a strong frame and symmetrical features. His face is deeply furrowed and His color about that of parchment. His carriage is erect and His entire form strikingly majestic and beautiful. His hands and nails are shapely and pure. His silver hair is long enough to touch the shoulders. The beard is snow white, the eyes light blue and penetrating, the nose slightly aquiline. The voice is powerful but capable of infinite pathos, tenderness and sympathy. His dress was that of the Oriental gentleman of the highest classes, simple and neat and very graceful. The color of His apparel was light, the outer robe being made of alpaca. On His head rested a light fez, surrounded by a white turban. The meekness of the servant, the majesty of the king, are in His brow and form."[5]

'Abdu'l-Baha's majesty was such that as Gregory approached him: "Following a natural impulse, my knee was bent reverently before Him. Feeling Him bend over me, I knew that He touched my head with his lips. He then raised me up and directed me to a seat. . . . I had never felt more peacwful or composed" than in the Master's presence.[6]

'Abdu'l-Bahá asked about the racial conflict in the United States. Gregory answered that those who had become Bahá'ís were more hopeful than others and that among them there were those who earnestly strove for racial unity. 'Abdu'l-Bahá asked if that was true for people of both races, and Gregory assured

'Abdu'l-Bahá walking on Mt. Carmel

him that such individuals were found in both races. He further explained that the central Bahá'í meeting was open to both races while other group meetings were organized along racial lines. 'Abdu'l-Bahá told him that there must be no distinction between races in the Bahá'í meetings. Their conversation went on for a while with Gregory feeling that—compared to the Master—even "... the tenderest parent could not have been so kind, patient, and understanding."[7]

At the next meeting, Gregory watched 'Abdu'l-Bahá being presented by his secretaries with letters and gifts from Bahá'ís in the United States. Gregory was happy to see what joy each gift—though small—brought to 'Abdu'l-Bahá because they represented the love of the Bahá'ís for him and by extension, the Faith. When again He and Gregory spoke about the unity of the races, 'Abdu'l-Bahá explained that the key was the acceptance of the Faith. All differences must eventually fade between believers. One way to do this was through intermarriage between the races. 'Abdu'l-Bahá repeated these points again the following day while receiving Gregory and again emphasized that all Bahá'í unity meetings must be open to Black people.

Gregory called on 'Abdu'l-Bahá at the Victoria Hotel and found him alone in his room, immersed in his correspondence:

> His smile of welcome was beautiful to see. He was occupied in looking over His correspondence, and for about an hour no one else came. It seemed a great privilege to be alone with Him, and I was impressed with His simplicity as never before. I also felt a longing for greater capacity to serve the Cause.[8]

When 'Abdu'l-Bahá's secretary arrived, Gregory was permitted to take notes on what he heard. The Master chanted a tablet noted down by the secretary and told Gregory to visit Cairo and Haifa and to speak to others so they could get to know him and hear from him. He also wanted Gregory to continue to teach among Black people as they would come into the Faith, and it would spread among them.

Before his departure from Ramleh, near Alexandria, Gregory visited 'Abdu'l-Bahá to take his leave. Among the visitors, he met the Master's grandsons including Shoghi, who later played such a big role in his life. Gregory told 'Abdu'l-Bahá that he had learned many valuable lessons that week. The Master replied that He hoped Gregory would come to understand that he didn't need a teacher—the Holy Spirit would guide him.

Through a storm, Gregory made his way from Alexandria to Jaffa near Jerusalem until they finally reached the Bay of Haifa at the foot of Mount Carmel. That evening, Gregory was invited to a

Thornton Chase with Mirza Abu'l-Fadl in Egypt, 1907

gathering in the home of 'Abdu'l-Bahá where twenty-five Persian Bahá'ís were present, many of whom made extraordinary sacrifices for the Faith including one man who had been the governor of a province in Persia and had given that up to be a Bahá'í and serve as Bahá'u'lláh's shepherd. Many of these individuals had spent considerable time with Bahá'u'lláh; meeting them was a rare bounty for Gregory. They stood up when their guest entered and greeted him warmly, asking him many questions about the progress of the Faith in America and the racial conditions there.

On the morning of the Holy Day of Ridvan, Gregory joined other pilgrims for dawn prayers and then went by carriage on a pilgrimage to the city of Akka wherein was the Most Great Prison. In this gloomy stone structure, the Holy Presence, Bahá'u'lláh, and 'Abdu'l-Bahá and the Holy family had been imprisoned in 1868 and suffered greatly. Their suffering, though, was full of deep meaning for the redemption of the world:

The Ancient Beauty hath consented to be bound with chains that mankind may be released from its bondage, and hath accepted to be made a prisoner within this most mighty Stronghold that the whole world may attain unto true liberty. He hath drained to its dregs the cup of sorrow, that all the peoples of the earth may attain unto abiding joy, and be filled with gladness. This is of the mercy of your Lord, the Compassionate, the Most Merciful. We have accepted to be abased, O believers in the Unity of God, that ye may be exalted, and have suffered manifold afflictions, that ye might prosper and flourish. He Who hath come to build anew the whole world, behold, how they that have joined partners with God have forced Him to dwell within the most desolate of cities![9]

From the prison, they made their way to the house in which Bahá'u'lláh had lived after His release. Removing their shoes, they entered His room. Gregory gazed on the portraits of the Báb and Bahá'u'lláh:

These faces are wonderful in their sublimity and beauty. Here is seen the expression of gentleness, meekness, wisdom, light, love, majesty, power, holiness, in short, every attribute of God which adorns the world of existence.[10]

For the final leg of the pilgrimage, they went by carriage out into the countryside to the mansion of Bahji and the Tomb of Bahá'u'lláh. In the tomb chamber, the pilgrims prayed: "Our earnest desire was for unity through the power of the Greatest Name." In the nearby Garden of Ridvan, pilgrims from Christian, Zoroastrian, and Muslim backgrounds gathered amid the trees, rivulet, fountain, and roses, for fellowship.

In one of his last encounters with 'Abdu'l-Bahá back in Egypt, Gregory was alone with him and one other believer:

The latter and I stood at one end of the room, while 'Abdu'l-Bahá in Majesty moved back and forth. The silence was deep but not oppressive, for Light and Cheer are radiated from this living Temple of Love. From the other end of the room in gentle tones He said in English, "Speak to Me, Mr. Gregory." I tried in vain to speak, to think of something to ask, of some want yet unsatisfied. But silent I remained, for my cup was full and running over. The feeling came to me that in order to receive larger gifts I must go out and work, that in His Providence the Giver of all might grant larger capacity.[11]

Before Gregory arrived for their last meeting, 'Abdu'l-Bahá exhorted Gregory to become the cause of guidance for many souls, to turn his face toward the kingdom and fear nothing.

Notes

1. The materials and quotations in this account of Louis Gregory's pilgrimage are from Louis Gregory, "A Heavenly Vista: The Pilgrimage of Louis Greogry," https://bahai-library.com/gregory_heavenly_vista, which should be considered as pilgrim's notes by the reader, unless indicated otherwise.
2. Gregory quoted in Morrison, *To Move the World*, 36.
3. Robert Turner, Phoebe Hearst's butler and first Black American Baha'í accompanied Mrs. Hearst and others on pilgrimage to the Holy Land to meet 'Abdu'l-Bahá in 1898.
4. Gregory quoted in Morrison, *To Move the World*, 36.
5. Gregory, "A Heavenly Vista."
6. Ibid.
7. Ibid.
8. Ibid.
9. Bahá'u'lláh, *Gleanings*, 99-100.
10. Gregory, "A Heavenly Vista."
11. Ibid.

'Abdu'l-Bahá with Lua Getsinger on the steps of the
home of Roy Wilhelm, 1912.

Chapter 8

'Abdu'l-Baha Goes to Washington

. . . . In view of the differences among the friends and the lack of unity . . . how can 'Abdu'l-Bahá hasten to those parts? . . . . If the friends . . . long for the visit of 'Abdu'l-Bahá they must immediately remove from their midst differences of opinion and be engaged in the practice of infinite love and unity . . . Now, we observe that strangeness, lack of unity and the utmost difference exists among the friend. . . . Under such a condition, how can they arise to guide the people of the world and establish union and harmony between the nations of the earth?. . . .[1]

For many years, Bahá'ís in America had asked 'Abdu'l-Bahá to come to visit their homeland. According to this tablet in early 1911 though, He perceived from their letters and visits a lack of true unity. Had they been able to establish that, the Faith would have spread like wildfire:

Verily, verily, I say unto you, were it not for this difference amongst you, the inhabitants of America in all those regions would have, by now, been attracted to the Kingdom of God, and would have constituted themselves your helpers and assisters . . . I beg of God to confirm you in union and concord that you may become the cause of the oneness of the kingdom of humanity.[2]

In the spring of 1912, the Master must have decided that the time had come to go to America. He had travelled through Western

Europe from August through December of 1911, infusing the Bahá'ís there with great faith. To the distress of his followers in Egypt who could not bear the physical separation, He again left despite his advanced age and physical condition. He boarded the *SS Cedric* which "became the bearer of the Most Holy Temple . . . and with great majesty and pride, it steamed out of Alexandria."[3]

On April 11th, the ship bearing 'Abdu'l-Bahá came into New York City harbor. He said that He had come ". . . to set forth in America the fundamental principles of the Revelation and Teachings of Bahá'u'lláh."[4]

His blessed presence arrived in Washington, D.C. by train on the afternoon of Saturday, April 20th. He appeared through the gates cloaked in his traditional Persian aba amid a flood of passengers to the great joy of a small band of his followers[5] which included two children, who offered him red roses and violets.[6]

'Abdu'l-Bahá was driven to the residence of Agnes Parsons, a red-brick Georgian mansion on the corner of R and 18th Streets, N.W. This was the first residence in which the Master lived while in the U.S. His custom was not to impose on people, but He knew that she had so looked forward to having him in her home that she'd made extensive preparations, and He didn't want to sadden her.

That evening, 'Abdu'l-Bahá spoke to a packed audience at a meeting of the Orient-Occidental Unity Conference.[7] The large audience rose to its feet as 'Abdu'l-Bahá entered and stayed standing until He gestured for everyone to be seated. He assured them that reciprocity and cooperation between Persia and America would yield great results. For human beings, ". . . cooperation and association are essential. Through association and meeting we find happiness and development, individual and collective."[8] America could be the cause of peace and cooperation throughout the world:

We will pray that the ensign of international peace may be uplifted and that the oneness of the world of humanity may be

realized and accomplished. All this is made possible and practicable through your efforts. May this American democracy
be the first nation to establish the foundation of international
agreement. May it be the first nation to proclaim the universality of mankind. May it be the first to upraise the standard of the
Most Great Peace, and through this nation of democracy may
these philanthropic intentions and institutions be spread and
broadcast throughout the world.[9]

The following day, April 21st, 'Abdu'l-Bahá explained to an
audience at Studio Hall, the local Bahá'í Center,[10] that bonds of
unity between people from faraway countries was accomplished
through the power of the Holy Spirit released by Bahá'u'lláh.
In this new cycle ". . . there will be an evolution in civilization
unparalleled in the history of the world." Humanity had been in
a "stage of infancy" but now:

> . . . the world of humanity in this cycle of its completeness and
> consummation will realize an immeasurable upward progress,
> and that power of accomplishment whereof each individual
> human reality is the depository of God—that outworking
> Universal Spirit—like the intellectual faculty, will reveal itself
> in infinite degrees of perfection.[11]

That afternoon, 'Abdu'l-Bahá spoke to a large audience at the
Universalist Church.[12] The Unitarian Universalist movement grew
out of the independent Congregational churches in Massachusetts
during the early days of the nation. Unlike traditional churches,
the Universalists do not profess a particular creed or focus on
specific doctrines or follow traditions but rather organize their
beliefs and lives around general principles such as the inherent
worth of every person, justice and equity, individual search for
truth, the interdependence of all life, and working for peace.

Following such principles led Universalists in being active
in social causes. Nevertheless, the church's invitation to 'Abdu'l-
Bahá to come and speak to the congregation drew criticism from

some that the church was giving a platform to a foreigner with a foreign faith who might share objectionable ideas. In introducing 'Abdu'l-Bahá, Rev. Dr. John Van Schaick, the pastor of the church, stated the importance of tolerance and the free exchange of views, even those that differed from one's own:

> What we in America need is the study of all religions. We need to learn what other nations have discovered: what all great prophets have proclaimed. If we dare not investigate others, it proves we have no men most willing to hear what others have to say. Those who will not listen to others are cowards. As we send missionaries to your country (addressing 'Abdu'l-Bahá), we ought to welcome the missionaries you send. Only by a free interchange of thought; only by sitting down and talking it over together; only by listening to all honest teachers, can world unity come.[13]

Standing before the full church, 'Abdu'l-Bahá said that superstitions and imitations had bound humanity in chains but that now, "We must investigate reality. We must put away these superstitions." The Manifestations of God had come to the world ". . . for the education of humanity, to develop immature souls into maturity, to transform the ignorant of mankind into the knowing, thereby establishing love and unity through divine education and training." All religions were in essence one reality and that through independent investigation people realize this, and there will be the ". . . basis for the oneness of the world of humanity."[14]

The parishioners were moved by what they heard and came one by one at a time meet 'Abdu'l-Bahá. So numerous were they that later He remarked teasingly, "the people in the church pressed my hand to such a degree that it is now aching." Back at the Parsons' residence, well-wishers came to meet 'Abdu'l-Bahá. Mr. Parsons suggested a visit to the Library of Congress to which 'Abdu'l-Bahá agreed. In the Library's magnificent rotunda, the Master was taking time to examine each bronze statue closely such that Mr. Parsons became concerned that the lights would be turned off. Just then, the building superintendent showed up and ordered that the lights be left on for the visitor.[15]

To a group of Bahá'ís[16] assembled in the Parsons home the next day, April 22nd, 'Abdu'l-Bahá recalled that when Bahá'u'lláh and His Family were exiled to Baghdad, they did not meet a single Bahá'í in any of the towns in villages. In Baghdad, there was but one Bahá'í and that today, there were Bahá'ís in the East and the West. The large meeting of Bahá'ís at the Parsons' home was evidence ". . . of how Bahá'u'lláh through the power of the love of God has exercised a wonderful spiritual influence throughout the world." He assured them that though the Bahá'í Movement had ". . . a very small, inconspicuous beginning. . . ," it would make ". . . sure and steady progress, gradually broadening and widening until it has assumed universal dimensions."[17]

When the Master had finished, a friend of Mrs. Parsons leaned over to her and said, "Isn't he a dear? I'm coming back tomorrow."[18]

Much of 'Abdu'l Bahá's days were spent meeting with individuals, listening to them, giving them guidance, and granting their various requests.[19] Mrs. Parsons hoped 'Abdu'l-Bahá would consent to watching her friend perform a dance she had choreographed to see if it had any moral value. He agreed—somewhat amusedly, saying that He had seen many things but never watched dancing.[20] After the performance, He "said it was good and blessed her work."[21]

With children, 'Abdu'l-Bahá was always solicitous of their well-being. One morning, He sat with Mrs. Parsons' young son, Jeffrey, for half an hour looking at his toys, books, and photos, before going up to the roof garden with him. Later that same morning, He met with families who attended the Bahá'í Sunday school. The parents brought their children forward to 'Abdu'l-Bahá who gave them a blessing in Persian.[22]

He made it a special point to greet each of the members of the household staff of the Parsons' residence. He spoke about the importance of being faithful and prayed for them, then He presented each staff member with a handmade silk handkerchief.[23]

For dinner that evening, Mirza Ahmad Sohrab prepared a full Persian meal. 'Abdu'l-Bahá served the guests personally and spoke with each of them. At the end of the meal, Mrs. Parsons invited the guests to come into the large room where a friend of hers[24] entertained everyone by playing the piano. 'Abdu'l-Bahá went into the small side room where He could eat his simple evening meal. Juliet Thompson, an artist from New York City, came in to speak with him and then others followed. Mr. Parsons had in his possession an old and beautifully embroidered traditional Persian outfit. Before the end of the evening, he asked Alice Barney—being a flamboyant dresser herself—to model it which she readily did. The Master looked up as Mrs. Barney entered, brightly arrayed, and laughed, exclaiming that the costume was very colorful.[25]

On April 23rd, at noon, 'Abdu'l-Bahá proclaimed the Bahá'í teachings to the largest number of Black Americans up to that time.

For several years, Louis Gregory, Coralie Franklin Cook, and other Bahá'ís were active in introducing the Bahá'í Faith to Black Americans and building relationships with prominent Black institutions and organizations. The Black-owned D.C. newspaper, the *Washington Bee,* noted that there was, at the time, ". . . quite a colony of colored Bahá'ists . . ." who were "earnest disciples." Louis Gregory was ". . . a brilliant young lawyer . . ." filled with "zeal," and the Bahá'í movement, one dedicated to "world-wide religious unity."[26] Gregory was an alumnus of Howard University, Cook taught there, and Bahá'í gatherings had been held on campus previously, so the meeting must have been much anticipated.

Many hundreds of people—mostly Black Americans—packed into Howard University's Rankin Chapel, a place of worship that would become known as a "beacon of non-denominational worship" and as a forum for speaking out about human rights.[27]

A band played music and the audience applauded exuberantly

Andrew Rankin Memorial Chapel, Howard University

to welcome 'Abdu'l-Bahá. The President of Howard University introduced their guest as the "Prophet of Peace and the harbinger of unity and salvation."[28]

The Master rose to speak:

> Today I am most happy, for I see here a gathering of the servants of God. I see white and black sitting together. There are no whites and blacks before God. All colors are one, and that is the color of servitude to God.[29]

What was the color of servitude to God? 'Abdu'l-Bahá had explained to Laura Barney during her pilgrimage that there were three degrees of existence. The first was that of Divinity—only God in His Essence dwelt at this degree. The second was Prophethood—these were God's Messengers who at all times manifested the attributes of God and taught and moved according to His Will alone. All human beings—irrespective of their status or background—were in the degree of servitude towards God.[30]

'Abdu'l-Bahá explained to the audience in the Rankin Chapel that ". . . in the realm of existence colors are of no importance." Even animals, ". . . despite the fact that they lack reason and understanding, do not make colors the cause of conflict. Why should man, who has reason, create conflict? This is wholly unworthy of him."[31] Every human being descended from common ancestors.

He hoped that the harmony at the gathering would increase to such a degree that "no distinctions shall remain." To reach this, there must be mutuality—both whites and Blacks must "strive jointly to make extraordinary progress and mix together completely," but to attain it would be ". . . impossible except through love."[32]

The Master's talk was much appreciated. Two long lines formed of people who came up to thank him afterward by doffing their hats and waving their kerchiefs.

From the Chapel, 'Abdu'l-Bahá was driven to the home of Ali Kuli Khan and Florence Khan for a luncheon.[33] Roses adorned the dining table around which 'Abdu'l-Bahá and nineteen guests sat.[34] 'Abdu'l-Bahá had sent a message earlier for Louis Gregory to come so they could meet there. When lunch was announced, 'Abdu'l-Bahá led all the guests in.

Louis Gregory stayed behind and waited for a good opportunity to leave as it was not the custom to have integrated meals. 'Abdu'l-Bahá soon noticed Gregory's absence at the table and insisted that a place be set for him to his right, the seat of honor.

Dining together has always had a greater significance than simply eating. The idea of "breaking bread" together is an indication of social equality and is, therefore, usually bound by specific rules. 'Abdu'l-Bahá's invitation to Gregory violated the unwritten rule that in the United States, Blacks and whites were not social equals and therefore must not break bread together. The situation on that day was an exact replica of the challenges faced by early Christians who also came from different backgrounds and strata of society and shared a common meal on worship day. Paul the Apostle explained to one community that: "There is neither Jew nor Greek, there is neither slave nor free, there is neither male nor female; for you are all one in Christ Jesus."

'Abdu'l-Bahá was teaching this same lesson to the early Bahá'ís of D.C.: that there was no black or white, no inferior or superior, no male nor female—all were united in the Covenant of Bahá'u'lláh. Nonessential realities were subsumed into a greater reality. The challenge for the early Christian community to whom Paul wrote was the same as the one faced by Bahá'ís: that in their day-to-day world, there *were* black and white, socially advantaged and disadvantaged, male and female. Bahá'ís had to transcend these categories through faith expressed in conscious action. The coming into being of a higher reality would require effort, as 'Abdu'l-Bahá explained in Paris:

> Bahá'u'lláh has drawn the circle of unity, He has made a design for the uniting of all the peoples, and for the gathering of them all under the shelter of the tent of universal unity. This is the work of the Divine Bounty, and we must all strive with heart and soul until we have the reality of unity in our midst, and as we work, so will strength be given unto us.[35]

In the circle of unity, all were included. This means that compassion for others extended beyond one's known circle. Eight days earlier the *Titanic*, the largest and sturdiest ship of its kind, sank to the astonishment of the world. Back at the Parsons' residence, 'Abdu'l-Bahá referred to this shocking tragedy to speak on the meaning of suffering. This disaster brought "distress to many souls." All things, though, have a wisdom and a reason which are shrouded in mystery. Though He felt sad for the loss of those who perished and for their families, He knew the "worlds of God are infinite" and that the deaths were the calling of many individuals from the temporary to the eternal. This world was like "the matrix of the mother from which a child is to be born into a spacious outer world." When the child leaves the womb, it finds that it has moved "from darkness into a sphere of radiance." After death, the soul is "released from the bondage of the limited to enjoy the liberties of the unlimited."[36]

That evening 'Abdu'l-Bahá went as a guest to a meeting of the Bethel Literary and Cultural Association, made up of Black American intelligentsia that met to hear talks about important issues of the day—especially those of direct concern to Black Americans—and discuss them. Among those in attendance was Leila Payne, who was so moved by what she heard that she became a Bahá'í and can be thought of as the first Black Bahá'í of Pittsburgh and, possibly, all of Pennsylvania.[37]

Before the large and learned audience of Black Americans, the Master praised the human being's unique capacity for intellectual investigation:

> Science is the first emanation from God toward man. All created beings embody the potentiality of material perfection, but the power of intellectual investigation and scientific acquisition is a higher virtue specialized to man alone.[38]

This capacity distinguished humans from the animal world, and with it, human beings can soar beyond the limits imposed on them by nature:

> All created things except man are captives of nature. The stars and suns swinging through infinite space, all earthly forms of life and existence—whether mineral, vegetable or animal—come under the dominion and control of natural law. Man through scientific knowledge and power rules nature and utilizes her laws to do his bidding. According to natural limitations he is a creature of earth, restricted to life upon its surface, but through scientific utilization of material laws he soars in the sky, sails upon the ocean, and dives beneath it.[39]

This great capacity was a blessing from God: "The truth is that God has endowed man with virtues, powers and ideal faculties of which nature is entirely bereft and by which man is elevated, distinguished and superior."[40] It could become the source of progress for a whole nation:

> The development and progress of a nation is according to the measure and degree of that nation's scientific attainments. Through this means its greatness is continually increased, and day by day the welfare and prosperity of its people are assured.[41]

And how should human beings use this capacity?

> By directing our efforts toward the unification of the human race. We must use these powers in establishing the oneness of the world of humanity, appreciate these virtues by accomplishing the unity of whites and blacks, devote this divine intelligence to the perfecting of amity and accord among all branches of the human family so that under the protection and providence of God the East and West may hold each other's hands and become as lovers. Then will mankind be as one nation, one race and kind . . .[42]

The next day, April 24th, 1912, 'Abdu'l-Bahá laid roses at the grave in Arlington Cemetery of Agnes Parsons' father who had fought in the Civil War.[43] He was then driven to Studio Hall where the Sunday School class was held. The two hundred mostly women and children awaited him in a room festooned with plants and cut flowers.[44] The children sang for him as He entered. He embraced each child. Jeffrey, Mrs. Parsons' son, said to his mother that it was like the story in the Bible about Jesus and the children.[45] 'Abdu'l-Bahá encouraged the mothers to "instill in their hearts the love of God" and "to acquire the divine perfections latent in the heart of man."[46]

To the many who had gathered back at the Parsons' residence,

'Abdu'l-Bahá expressed the hope that "these gatherings may be productive of great results" and that:

> ... there is no greater result than the love of God. There is no greater result than bonds of service in the divine Kingdom and attainment to the good pleasure of the Lord. Therefore, I desire that your hearts may be directed to the Kingdom of God, that your intentions may be pure and sincere, your purposes turned toward altruistic accomplishment unmindful of your own welfare; nay, rather, may all your intentions center in the welfare of humanity, and may you seek to sacrifice yourselves in the pathway of devotion to mankind.[47]

He promised them that:

> If you arise in the Cause of God with divine power, heavenly grace, the sincerity of the Kingdom, a merciful heart and decisive intention, it is certain that the world of humanity will be entirely illumined, the moralities of mankind will become merciful, the foundations of the Most Great Peace will be laid, and the oneness of the kingdom of man will become a reality.[48]

After the meeting, Agnes Parsons had tea brought to 'Abdu'l-Bahá. When the cup was poured for him, He handed it to her.[49]

That evening, 'Abdu'l-Bahá spoke to another interracial group, this time at the home of the Dyers. He expressed his delight at seeing the diversity of people and explained that in the world of nature, existence was the result of elements combining whereas division and disintegration resulted in non-existence. So it was in the human world. When the elements were all combined, the beauty of the whole could be seen. When Black and white people were united, "the composite beauty of humanity will be witnessed in their unity and blending."[50]

This unity was God's Will: "The Prophets of God were sent into the world upon this mission of unity and agreement: that these long-separated sheep might flock together."[51]

'Abdu'l-Bahá promised this:

When the racial elements of the American nation unite in actual fellowship and accord, the lights of the oneness of humanity will shine, the day of eternal glory and bliss will dawn, the spirit of God encompass, and the divine favors descend. Under the leadership and training of God, the real Shepherd, all will be protected and preserved. He will lead them in green pastures of happiness and sustenance, and they will attain to the real goal of existence. This is the blessing and benefit of unity; this is the outcome of love. This is the sign of the Most Great Peace; this is the star of the oneness of the human world.[52]

The meeting that evening at the Dyers was filled with spirit. Before arriving 'Abdu'l-Bahá was tired but "at the sight of such genuine love and attraction between the white and the Black friends, I was so moved that I spoke with great love and affection. . . ."[53] Afterwards, while walking down the street, 'Abdu'l-Bahá raised his voice in praise:

O Bahá'u'lláh! May my life be sacrificed for Thee! O Bahá'u'lláh! May my soul be offered up for Thy sake! How full were Thy days with trials and tribulations! How severe the ordeals Thou didst endure! How solid the foundation Thou hast finally laid, and how glorious the banner Thou didst hoist![54]

Later that evening, 'Abdu'l-Bahá attended a meeting of the scientific society[55] headed by the great inventor, Alexander Graham Bell, who had invited him to attend. Bell had an extraordinarily creative mind and a relentless drive for working towards new discoveries, never sitting still on one breakthrough. He was one of the inventors of telephone technology and the first to patent a practical telephone technology, he then founded AT&T, thereby launching the telecommunications industry. He also invented and tested the first wireless communications device—the photophone, the hydro-airplane, an early form of metal detection,

Inventor Alexander Graham Bell

as well as making early discoveries in the recording of sound. In his office, he rigged up an early form of air conditioning and experimented on his property with renewable energy such as solar power and compost toilets. He was greatly motivated in his altruistic effort to help the deaf connect to the hearing world because his mother, sister, and wife were all deaf. Though most of his life was spent pursuing a wide array of scientific studies, he described himself as a "teacher of the deaf."

'Abdu'l-Bahá entered the gathering in Bell's home and the guests interrupted their discussion of scientific matters and stood to greet him. At the end of the discussion, Bell asked Ali Kuli Khan to talk to them about the history of the Faith. Bell then invited

'Abdu'l-Bahá to speak to the group. To this group of scientific thinkers and enthusiasts, 'Abdu'l-Bahá praised the importance of science and its beneficial results. He described the new Revelation in exalted terms, greatly moving the audience such that afterwards Bell found himself "inadequate to say anything."[56]

In the pre-World War I years, there was great interest among Americans and Europeans in new spiritual belief systems such as Theosophy and new internationalist efforts such as the invention of the Esperanto language. The day after his visit to the Bell home, 'Abdu'l-Bahá spoke at the Parsons' home to practitioners of each of these groups.

Theosophy was a new religious movement and philosophy developed by Helena Blavatsky, a Russian Immigrant to the U.S. Among its teachings are that the material world is an emanation from God and that the purpose of human life is for the soul to break the bonds of this material world. 'Abdu'l-Bahá explained to the Theosophists that "the greatest power in the realm and range of human existence is spirit—the divine breath which animates and pervades all things."[57]

This spirit manifests itself to different degrees at different levels of existence. Spirit is manifested in vegetables as growth, in animals as sense perception, and in humans as the power of reflection and ideation—the human mind can bring the invisible into the visible and make the unknown known. But every level of creation is limited to itself—plants cannot understand animals, nor animals humans. Such is it with human beings and the Divine Worlds of the Kingdom of God. Human beings can, though, receive the Divine Spirit of that Kingdom which emanates like rays from God, the Sun of Reality. While human beings are not in God nor God in them—the Divine Essence can never be divided—they can be the recipients of this Divine Spirit, the outpouring of which is unceasing. With this Divine Spirit, human beings go beyond mere material existence and make spiritual progress which is the true purpose of life:

> We must strive unceasingly and without rest to accomplish the development of the spiritual nature in man, and endeavor with tireless energy to advance humanity toward the nobility of its true and intended station.[58]

Esperantists were people interested in the study and spread of Esperanto, a constructed international language created by the Polish Jewish doctor, L. L. Zamenhof, in the late 1800s. To the group of Esperantists gathered at the Parsons' home, 'Abdu'l-Bahá asserted that:

> Unless the unity of languages is realized, the Most Great Peace and the oneness of the human world cannot be effectively organized and established because the function   of language is to portray the mysteries and secrets of human hearts.[59]

The creation of a universal auxiliary language would permit the transmission of knowledge of the Divine Teachings throughout the world. Thereby becoming "the cause of the tranquility of the human commonwealth."[60]

Many of the guests wanted to meet 'Abdu'l-Bahá individually so they stayed after his talks. Throughout this day, as with others, there was a constant stream of visitors such that 'Abdu'l-Bahá acknowledged the patience and hospitality of Mrs. Parsons by referring to himself and saying that "such a traveler and guest is the cause of much bother . . . you have had to host the public from morning until evening."[61] Among the visitors were Charles and Mariam Haney and their three-year-old son. The Haneys had been on pilgrimage in 1909 while she was pregnant. When the little boy saw 'Abdu'l-Bahá on this visit, he screamed, which Mariam attributed to his keen awareness of the station of the Master.[62] He had been in the Master's presence while still in the embryonic stage. After his birth, 'Abdu'l-Bahá gave him the name 'Paul' in a letter.[63] He grew up into a devoted Bahá'í, later appointed a Hand of the Cause by Shoghi Effendi.

To the afternoon group at the Parsons' home that day, 'Abdu'l-Bahá explained how the Divine Teachings became clouded over with time by "imitations and superstitions." Then the "Sun of Truth, the Word of God" rises again." Therefore:

> The first teaching of Bahá'u'lláh is the duty incumbent upon all to investigate reality. What does it mean to investigate reality? It means that man must forget all hearsay and examine truth himself, for he does not know whether statements he hears are in accordance with reality or not. Wherever he finds truth or reality, he must hold to it, forsaking, discarding all else; for outside of reality there is naught but superstition and imagination.[64]

'Abdu'l-Bahá then went to speak with guests at the home of Mrs. Barney and then of Mrs. Khan, and from there was brought by the Parsons to a dinner at the Turkish Embassy in his honor. The dinner was formal, with roses on the table in front of 'Abdu'-Baha's seat and the guests in their best attire.[65]

For four decades, 'Abdu'l-Bahá had been a prisoner of the Ottoman Turkish Empire, and now here He was in the Embassy of Turkey in a faraway and completely foreign land, and the Turkish Ambassador stood and honored him:

> The light of His honor's quality and knowledge in this new land and new world is now shining upon all peoples. . . . He has suffered and sacrificed everything for the purpose of disseminating good qualities for humanity. . . .[66]

'Abdu'l-Baha then spoke not of his time as a prisoner and his years of suffering, but of the oneness of humanity. It was evident now that all peoples were related, all were from one family and citizens of one country. The purpose of the Manifestations of God had always been to educate humanity in the truth and the truth

'Abdu'l-Bahá at the home of Agnes Parsons in Washington, D.C. where most of the meetings occurred during His visits to Washington and which still stands today at 1700 18th Street NW.

was one, not plural. The differences between peoples were due to the imitation of the traditions of the past. These could be let go and the Sun of Reality would emerge.[67]

During the last two and half days of 'Abdu'l-Bahá's stay in Washington, D.C., He continued to speak to large groups in public and meet with individuals who came to both meet this extraordinary man for themselves and seek his guidance and learn from his spiritual insights.[68] To these groups, He related teachings of Bahá'u'lláh to contemporary issues. To individuals, He always offered encouragement and praised each one for some good quality they possessed or for something they had accomplished.

The *Washington Bee*, the D.C.-based weekly paper founded by Black Americans, noted the "unusual" nature of the meetings—they included both white and Black Americans:

> Its [the Bahá'í Faith's] white devotees, even in this prejudice-ridden community, refuse to draw the color line. The informal meetings, held frequently in the fashionable mansions of the cultured society in Sheridan Circle, Dupont Circle, Connecticut and Massachusetts avenues, have been open to Negroes on terms of absolute equality.[69]

On Friday morning, April 26th, 'Abdu'l-Bahá spoke before the Woman's Alliance at All-Souls Unitarian Church on equal rights for men and women.[70] The audience greatly appreciated his remarks, and He was so pleased with the spirit of the gathering that He later cabled that "today three-thousand persons visited in utmost harmony."[71] From there, 'Abdu'l-Bahá walked to the home of Mrs. John J. White who had asked him to come and speak to her at her home; Mrs. Parsons offered him a carriage but He preferred to walk.

Later at the Parsons' residence, the Turkish Ambassador came for lunch and spoke animatedly with 'Abdu'l-Bahá for a longtime in Turkish. Mrs. Parsons asked Dr. Farid about translating, and he answered that he had not been told to do so.[72] The Persian assistants who travelled with 'Abdu'l-Bahá had both a spiritual and a historical sense of the station of the Master and were mindful not to presume anything about him or impose themselves in any way.

After more personal visits, the main room at the Parsons filled up for the late afternoon meeting at which 'Abdu'l-Bahá spoke on what it meant to be created in the image of God.[73] He encouraged the audience to learn from the teachings. Once the audience left, 'Abdu'l-Bahá gave some time to meeting with Mrs. Parsons during which He spoke with her about her husband and son, presumably to encourage and guide her and them.[74]

The Bahá'ís of D.C. had planned a large public meeting for that evening and the only hall large enough to meet the demand was the Daughters of the American Revolution's Constitution Hall. This organization began in the late 1800s when there was a renewed interest in the colonial period and the nation's origins. Most patriotic and historical associations were male so women wanted to found one so they could hold their own programs devoted to the celebration and preservation of the nation's history. DAR Constitution Hall was the largest hall in D.C. at the time.

The Master spoke of the beauty of the building in which they stood as a proof of the advancement of women and explained that the equality of men and women was a teaching of Bahá'u'lláh.

Other prominent citizens[75] spoke from the rostrum including Samuel Gompers, a major figure in organizing labor to protect workers from gross exploitation by large business owners, a major issue during those decades when unsanitary and dangerous working conditions coupled with low wages were common. Gompers founded the American Federation of Labor and worked to harmonize the interests of various labor groups to create a large voting block capable of creating systemic change. When meeting the Master, Gompers said that he tried to do his duty. The Master affirmed his efforts and encouraged him indirectly by saying that if everyone did their duty, there would be no labor issues.[76] Though the meeting was held in a building built by women for an organization founded and run by women, there were no women speakers as women speaking in public was exceedingly rare in those days, a sign that the equality of men and women had yet to be realized.

The following day, two women from prominent families, Mrs. Katherine Nourse and Mrs. Elise Cabot, came to meet 'Abdu'l-Bahá.[77] The Parsons moved in powerful and moneyed circles. Mrs. Parsons that morning had offered 'Abdu'l-Bahá funds but He told her that He did not travel without being able to pay for it and encouraged her to give the funds to the poor.

At lunch, 'Abdu'l-Bahá spoke to the guests—who included Franklin MacVeigh, the Secretary of the Treasury—about wealth in society and the issue of progressive taxation.[78] This idea generally meant that the more profit a person had at the end of a year, the more taxes they should pay into a common fund. This money in common, then, can be allocated to those in need so that there won't be great extremes of wealth and poverty, which is unjust and the cause of unrest.[79]

For 'Abdu'l-Bahá's last evening in D.C., Mrs. Parsons held a grand reception for several hundred prominent Washingtonians including senators, statesmen, and even a justice of the Supreme Court. This dinner was given under the auspices of the Persian-American Educational Society.[80] Before and after the dinner, the Master spoke with each person who approached him. To every one of them, He made encouraging remarks and gave them a grander vision to which they could aspire. To a judge, He said the countries of the world could unify as the states had in America.[81]

To doctors, He said He hoped they could raise the standard of universal peace.

To a member of Congress, He said that just as He was expending himself on the good of the nation, He hoped he would expend himself on the good of the world as well.

To a bishop, He said He hoped he would abandon harmful

imitation, teach the true teachings of Christ, and let go of dogmas.

To Admiral Peary, He said He hoped he would discover the mysteries of the Kingdom of God.[82]

On the last day of his first visit to Washington, D.C., April 28, 1912, 'Abdu'l Baha received a few seekers and well-wishers and called on the Turkish Ambassador.[83] To one of the men who came, the Master explained that a man must not retaliate, rather it is up to the law of a country to carry out a punishment. This punishment should never be in the spirit of revenge.

Later, in the carriage on the way to the train station, Abdu'l-Baha passed Sheridan Circle with Mrs. Parsons, where her son Jeffrey was playing with friends. At the station, a group had gathered to catch a few more moments with 'Abdu'l-Bahá and see him off to Chicago.[84]

Before leaving, the Master assured Mrs. Parsons:

This was the springtime; we had good meetings at your home; I shall never forget them. I shall pray for divine confirmation for you that you may be assisted both materially and spiritually. This material world has an outward appearance, as it has also an inner reality. All created things are interlinked in a chain leading to spirituality and ultimately ending in abstract realities. I hope that these spiritual links will become stronger day by day and that this communication of hearts, which is termed inspiration, will continue. When this connection exists, bodily separation is not important; this condition is beyond the world of words and above all description.[85]

To the others, 'Abdu'l-Bahá said: "I hope these meetings of ours will bring forth everlasting results. The greatest of all benefits is the oneness of humanity and universal peace."[86]

Notes

1. Allan Ward, *239 Days*, 4-5.
2. Ibid.
3. Mahmud Zarqani, quoted in ibid., 9.
4. 'Abdu'l-Bahá, *The Promulgation of Universal Peace*, i.
5. Mason Remey, Mirza Ahmad Sohrab, Joseph Hannen, Mirza Ali Kuli Khan, and Florence Khan, and their two children, Rahim and Marzieh, Alice Barney. 'Abdu'l-Bahá was accompanied on the train by his Persian assistants Mahmud Zarqani, Mirza Valiyu'llah Nakhjavani, and Dr. Amin Farid (Parsons, Diary, 9-10). Travelling with 'Abdu'l-Bahá on the train also were Dr. Edward Getsinger, who had begged 'Abdu'l-Bahá to be allowed to go with him, and John Bosch from California (Zarqani, *Mahmud's Diary*, 48-49).
6. Marzieh Gail, *Arches of the Years*, 79.
7. The Orient-Occidental Unity Conference is described in the Parsons Diary (11, footnote 12) as "a gathering of the Persian-American Educational Society"; Hannen describes it as "the third and final session of the Orient-Occidental Unity" (Hannen, "'Abdu'l-Bahá in Washington DC," 7). The Persian-American Educational Society was founded by Ahmad Sohrab to build bridges between the U.S. and Persia and help educational efforts. Laura Barney was an active contributor to the society, donating up to $1,100 for scholarships for boys in Persia ("Persian-American Educational Society," v. 1, n. 1, 13). Her mother served as an honorary vice-president and was instrumental to the success of the society. She was able to involve Sidney Sprague, a former Harvard professor, in the effort. In 1908, he became the headmaster of the Tarbiyat School for Boys, a Bahá'í-run school in Tehran (Mona Khademi, *The Life of Laura Clifford Barney*, Oxford: George Ronald, 2022.). 'Abdu'l-Bahá suggested that the name be changed to Persian-American Interdependence Society so that the work of the organization could include other fields in addition to education such as commerce. In the same Tablet, 'Abdu'l-Bahá refers to the organization as the 'Oriental-Occidental Interdependence Society' ("The Persian-American Educational Society," v.1, n. 5, 4-6). Judging from subsequent correspondence, the name change did not happen.
8. 'Abdu'l-Bahá, *The Promulgation of Universal Peace*, 35.
9. 'Ibid., 36-37.
10. Gareissen Studio Hall located at 1219 Connecticut Ave. N.W., served as the D.C. Bahá'í Center: "The Bahá'í Assembly of Washington, D. C., holds its meetings on Friday evenings at 8 o'clock, at the Gareissen Studio, 1219 Connecticut avenue, N.W. This Studio, which has been our headquarters since December 1, 1909, is well located and commodious,

having a seating capacity of about 200. The weekly meetings are well attended, and interest is growing constantly. In addition to the Friday meetings, there is a Sunday school, with classes for children and an adult department, which meets at 11:15 Sunday mornings, for the study of Bible prophecies and of the Ishrakat, Tarazat, Tajalleyat and Tablet of Paradise. The Unity Feasts are observed on the appointed dates, generally at the Studio, the rental of which covers all of these meetings." (Hannen, "Washington, D.C.," Bahá'í News, v. I, n. I, 18). Parsons (Diary, 14) cites 'Studio Hall' as being in 'Studio House', Alice Barney's home. But her home was at 2306 Massachusetts Ave, N.W., D.C., and Studio Hall, as listed in *The Promulgation of Universal Peace*, was at 1219 Connecticut Ave, N.W., D.C.

11. 'Abdu'l-Bahá, *The Promulgation of Universal Peace*, 38.

12. Located at 13th and L St. N.W., Washington, D.C. (Hannen, "'Abdu'l-Bahá in Washington, D.C." *Star of the West*, 6).

13. Rev. Dr. Van Schaick quoted in "'Abdu'l-Bahá talks of Universal Peace."

14. 'Abdu'l-Bahá, *The Promulgation of Universal Peace*, 40-42.

15. Parsons, *Diaries*, 19-20.

16. Hannen notes that the following were seated for "supper" and that 'Abdu'l-Bahá served them: "'Abdu'l-Bahá Abbas, Dr. Ameen U. Fareed, Mirza Ali Kuli Khan, Mirza Ali Akbar Khan, Seyad Assad Ullah, Mirza Mahmood, Mirza Ahmad Sohrab, Dr. E.C. Getsinger, Charles Mason Remey, Joseph H. Hannen" ("'Abdu'l-Bahá in Washington, D.C." *Star of the West*, v. 3, n. 3, 12).

17. 'Abdu'l-Bahá, *The Promulgation of Universal Peace*, 43-44.

18. Mrs. Richardson quoted in Parsons, *Diary*, 23. Parsons also introduced Mrs. Buckner Randolph (see f. 172) and Ms. Eliza Hay to 'Abdu'l-Bahá. Hay lived at 1304 9th St., N.W., D.C. (Parsons, *Diary*, 148).

19. According to Agnes Parsons (*Diary*, 13), a typical day would be: "7 A.M. Tea and bread, 1:30 P.M. Dines with family, 4 P.M. Tea, 7:30 P.M. sits with family at dinner but partakes of no food himself, 10 P.M. simple meal." Sometimes He dictated or read correspondence at the evening meal.

20. In the Near East, it would have been a very surprising request to ask a man to sit privately and watch a woman to whom he was not related, dance, much a less man of 'Abdu'l-Bahá's station.

21. Parsons, *Diary*, 16.

22. Ibid., 14.

23. Ibid, 22.

24. Mrs. Randolph (Ibid., 26) was an accomplished pianist and was married to Dr. Buckner Magill Randolph who practiced in Parsons' neighborhood.

25. Ibid., 27.

26. *The Washington Bee*, 27 April, 1912, quoted in Morrison, *To Move the World*, 51.

27. "This beautiful and historic building has been graced by African American heroes such as Frederick Douglass, Mary McLeod Bethune, W. E. B. DuBois and Benjamin E. Mays; outstanding national and foreign leaders, such as John F. Kennedy, Eleanor Roosevelt, William Jefferson Clinton, Haile Selassie I, and Desmond Tutu; and, of course, the most distinguished American preachers such as Vernon Johns, Martin Luther King, Jr., Samuel Proctor, Gardner Taylor, William Holmes Borders, Reinhold Niebuhr, and Howard Thurman." ("History and Legacy")

28. Zarqani, *Mahmud's Diary*, 55.

29. 'Abdu'l-Bahá, *The Promulgation of Universal Peace*, 45.

30. 'Abdu'l-Bahá, *Some Answered Questions*, 230.

31. 'Abdu'l-Bahá, *The Promulgation of Universal Peace*, 45.

32. Ibid., 46.

33. The Persian Legation was located at 1832 16th Street, N.W., Washington, D.C.

34. These included the Khans and their two children; Mrs. Breed, Florence Khan's mother; Mrs. Severance; Mrs. Goodall; Mrs. Cooper; Ms. A. Dorr, an acquaintance of Alice Barney-Hemnick (Parsons, Diary, 146); Dr. Edward Getsinger; Dr. Amin Farid; Mirza Sohrab; Juliet Thompson; Louis Gregory; Charles Mason Remey; and Agnes Parsons (Parsons, Diary, 31) and "members of the official and social life of Washington" (Ober, *Bahá'í World*, v. 12). After lunch, 'Abdu'l-Bahá was invited into an upper room in the Khan home where He spoke to several distinguished guests including the arctic explorer, Admiral Peary, (Parsons, *Diary*, 35), Alexander Graham Bell (Zarqani, *Mahmud's diary*, 57), and an "Italian duke" (Gregory, *Early Days*, 13). Peary claimed to have reached the North Pole in 1909 after much exploration.

35. 'Abdu'l-Bahá, *Paris Talks*, 54.

36. 'Abdu'l-Bahá, *The Promulgation of Universal Peace*, 46-48.

37. For more information about Leila Payne and her life of service as a community leader, see "Leila Young Payne."

38. 'Abdu'l-Bahá, *The Promulgation of Universal Peace*, 49.

39. Ibid., 49.

40. Ibid., 51.

41. Ibid., 49.

42. Ibid., 61.

43. Mrs. Parsons father was William B. Royall. He served in the military as an officer for more than forty years. He was a very good soldier and commander, fighting in battles like Battle of Hanover C.H. Virginia and

Old Church Virginia and against the Native Americans on Rosebud Creek Montana. In his years of service, he moved up the ranks quickly, he was a Colonel Brevet Brigadier General when he retired from disability in 1887. He died on December 13, 1895 ("William Bedford Royall").

44. Hannen, "Washington D.C.," 7.
45. Parsons, *Diary*, 41-42.
46. 'Abdu'l-Bahá, The Promulgation of Universal Peace, 53.
47. Ibid., 54.
48. Ibid, 55.
49. Parsons, *Diary*, 43.
50. 'Abdu'l-Bahá, *The Promulgation of Universal Peace*, 57.
51. Ibid.
52. Ibid.
53. Zarqani, *Mahmud's Diary*, 57.
54. 'Abdu'l-Bahá quoted in Shoghi Effendi, *God Passes By*, 292.
55. This is Zarqani's description of the gathering in Bell's home. Across the street was the Volta Bureau where Bell and others conducted their research into deafness and developed educational strategies for it as well as other scientific experiments. The meeting which 'Abdu'l-Bahá attended may have been people associated with the work of the Bureau or members of the National Geographic Society, of which Bell had been the President.
56. Alexander Graham Bell quoted in Zarqani, *Mahmud's Diary*, 58.
57. 'Abdu'l-Bahá, *The Promulgation of Universal Peace*, 58.
58. Ibid., 60.
59. Ibid., 60.
60. Ibid., 61.
61. Zarqani, *Mahmud's Diary*, 59.
62. Parsons, *Diary*, 46.
63. *The Bahá'í World*, vol. XVIII, p. 614.
64. 'Abdu'l-Bahá, *The Promulgation of Universal Peace*, 62. At some point that afternoon, 'Abdu'l-Bahá spoke with "Miss Evelyn Bailey, Mrs. Wells, Miss Anne Wells, and Miss Larkin of England." He was driven to the home of Mrs. Barney-Hemnick and Mrs. Khan by Mrs. Sallie Jacobs Elkins (Parsons, *Diary*, 47). Nothing is known to the authors of these individuals.
65. According to *Mahmud's Diary*, there were "many dignitaries" (60) and according to Agnes Parsons, the guests were: "the Ambassador, his son, his son's wife, his daughter, Mirza and Mme. Khan, Dr. and Mrs. Williams, Dr. Fareed, the two visiting Persians, the Persian Secretary, Mr. Parsons, and myself." (*Diary*, 47)
66. Zarqani, *Mahmud's Diary*, 60.

67. 'Abdu'l-Bahá paraphrased from notes in Zarqani, *Mahmud's Diary*, 60-61.

68. Exact transcriptions of 'Abdu'l-Bahá's talks during the last three days have not been published or are not extant.

69. *The Washington Bee*, April 27th, 1912, quoted in Ward, *239 Days*, 37.

70. This is according to Zia Baghdadi, "'Abdu'l-Bahá in America," *Star of the West*, v. 19, n. 3, 91. According to Zarqani, (*Mahmud's Diary*, 62), "the Master spoke on the subject of the varieties of light, the effulgence, of the Sun of Reality in its original essence, and of the waiting souls with pure hearts who are like unto clear spotless mirrors, whose eyes and ears become enlightened by the appearance of the Sun of Reality." We have gone with Baghdadi's version because, according to the introduction of the article, the notes were checked by 'Abdu'l-Bahá.

71. Zarqani, *Mahmud's Diary*, 62.

72. Parsons, *Diary*, 50-51.

73. Zarqani writes that the talk was "the interpretation of the Old Testament statement concerning the creation of man in the image of God," *Mahmud's Diary*, 62. Parsons (*Diary*, 51) writes that the talk was on "the Human and Divine Spirit in Man."

74. Parsons, *Diary*, 51.

75. Ibid., 52. These included William Hoar, a Bahá'í and President of the Persian-American Educational Society; Mr. Kraemer, Superintendent of Public Schools; and Mr. Arthur C. Monahan from the Bureau of Education.

76. Ibid.

77. The Cabots built a fortune in shipping and then went into politics. Elise Cabot was married to Thomas Handasyd Cabot of Boston, MA. The couple had a home in Dublin, New Hampshire, where Parsons summered too and which is where the two got to know each other (Ibid., 145). Parsons gives no indication that Katherine Nourse was a Bahá'í. She may have been related to the famous Nourse family which counted as an ancestor Joseph Nourse, one of the founders of the Treasury Department. The family members owned homes on properties that became Dumbarton Oaks, the St. Alban's School, and the Sidwell Friends School. They were slave owners before the Civil War which divided the family as it did the nation (Auslander, "They Knew This Land"). Joseph Nourse's family tree does not indicate a "Katherine." There was a "Catharine" Nourse who was a Bahá'í child (b.1904) who later pioneered to Hawaii ("Catharine E. Nourse 1904—1985").

78. Zarqani (*Mahmud's Diary*, 64). Parsons (*Diary*, 53) does not mention him by name as being there. Ward (*239 Days*, 45) describes the encounter as taking place at breakfast but does not give a reference.

79. If any notes were taken at that luncheon by Dr. Farid (Parsons, *Diary*, 54), they are either not extant or have never been published. For 'Abdu'l-Bahá's views on progressive taxation, see 'Abdu'l-Bahá, *Foundations for World Unity*, 38-43.

80. Hannen, "'Abdu'l-Bahá in Washington, D.C.," *Star of the West*, v. 3, n. 3, 7. Baghdadi ("'Abdu'l-Bahá in America," 91) describes it as being at the "luncheon hour." Zarqani (*Mahmud's Diary*, 65) describes it as being on behalf of the 'Orient-Occident Society.'

81. Baghdadi describe him as a judge of the Supreme Court, Zarqani as a "Washington judge." Zarqani (*Mahmud's Diary*, 64-5) states that among the guests were: the head of the US Patent Office, the President of the Peace Congress, relatives of President Taft, and the Charge d'Affaires from the Embassy of Switzerland—Baghdadi ("'Abdu'l-Bahá in America," 91) describes him as the 'Ambassador'. Edward Bruce Moore, the head of the US Patent Office, was appointed by President Taft in 1911 as chairman of the American delegation to the Conference of the International Union for the Protection of Industrial Property, which met in Washington, D.C., and at which forty nations were represented ("Edward Bruce Moore").

The President of the Peace Congress may have been Henry L. Stimson who was serving as President Taft's Secretary of War (Kraft, *Some Must Dream*). Both men were committed to the cause of international peace and the development of international structures for arbitration and peace. Stimson served twice as secretary of War and once of State. He lived to see the Atomic Age and continued to advocate for mechanisms to create and sustain international peace. Charles Mason Remey spoke about the Bahá'í Faith at the Peace Congress of 1911.

Parsons (*Diary*, 55) names the following guests:
General Adolphus Greely was a former Civil War veteran who was wounded three times and accepted an officer commission with the 81st, a division of Black soldiers. He later led a weather expedition to the Arctic where he survived three winters and was one of seven in the expedition to come back alive. He was one of the founders of the National Geographic Society and the first free public library in the country ("Fire and Ice: Adolphus W. Greely").

Admiral Wainwright came from a longtime Naval family and served with distinction as a ship's commander in the Spanish-American War. He was an officer on the USS Maine when it blew up and sank; the false news stories that were promoted about this incident and the sinking itself were contributing factors to the outbreak of the war ("Wainwright to Leave the Navy").

Mrs. Sherman Niles: biographical information unknown to authors.

82. Zarqani, *Mahmud's Diary*, 64-65.

83. Edward Alfred Mitchell Innes worked at the British Embassy. He was not, contrary to what Zarqani writes, the British ambassador (*Mahmud's Diary*, 66, f. 66). According to Parsons (*Diary*, 57-58), those who came that day were Mr. and Mrs. William Karney Carr, Dr. Chase, and Mr. Innes. Dr. Chase was a dentist who lived at 1522 K St., N.W., D.C. (Parsons, *Diary*, 146).

Mr. Innes may refer to Alfred-Mitchell Innes who served as the Counselor at the British Embassy in Washington, D.C. from 1908 to 1913. He was a gifted economist and wrote "the best pair of articles on the nature of money written in the twentieth century" (Wray, *Credit and state theories*, 223) On the way to the station, the Master and Mrs. Parsons stopped at the home of Mrs. John J. White to say goodbye. She was delighted to have another chance to speak with 'Abdu'l-Bahá (Parsons, *Diary*, 58).

84. According to Parsons (*Diary*, 58), those at the train station were the Turkish Ambassador and his son, Mirza and Mme. Khan, Mirza Sohrab, Mr. Remey, Mrs. Belmont, Leona [Barnitz] and two or three others. Barnitz was a Bahá'í of D.C. who served for years as the Bahá'í community's archivist. She preserved Parsons' Diary which recounts much of 'Abdu'l-Bahá's visit to Washington D.C. (Parsons, *Diary*, 144). She served as Parsons' personal secretary (Moe, *Aflame with Devotion*, 33). Mrs. Belmont and her husband Arnold Belmont were most likely D.C. Bahá'ís. They assisted at the time of 'Abdu'l-Bahá's visit: "They are both here anxious to do some service for 'Abdu'l-Bahá. Mr. Belmont answers the telephone and the "little girl" conducts the visitors to 'Abdu'l-Bahá's room for interviews, keeping a list of the names" ("The First Nine Days," 15). In Egypt, 'Abdu'l-Bahá heard news of the D.C. Bahá'ís and Mrs. Belmont: "The third monthly report of Mr. Joseph H. Hannen, from Washington, D.C., was read. As He listened, He exclaimed "Bravo Mrs. Belmont," "Bravo So and So." . . . In the evening He told the believers that a good report had been received from Washington which made him very happy" (*'Abdu'l-Bahá in Egypt*, 236). On the morning of April 27th, Mrs. Belmont fit 'Abdu'l-Bahá for a coat which she made for him (Parsons, *Diary*, 53).

85. Zarqani, *Mahmud's Diary*, 66. Parsons states (*Diary*, 59) that "'Abdu'l-Bahá assured me He would be with us, although He was going to Chicago".

86. 'Abdu'l-Bahá quoted in Zarqani, *Mahmud's Diary*, 66.

Wedding photo of Louis and Louise Mathew Gregory

Chapter 9

Louis Gregory and Louise Mathew Marry

A fter Washington, D.C., 'Abdu'l-Bahá traveled to Chicago. These were two cities in the U.S. with large populations of Black Americans. During his talks in those cities, 'Abdu'l-Bahá proclaimed the teachings of Bahá'u'lláh to many educated Black Americans and firmly implanted in them a positive impression of the Faith.

At a public meeting following the Convention of the Bahá'í Temple Unity, the national group formed in 1909 with the goal of building a House of Worship in the United States, He explained that, in a sense, the physical temple was a metaphor:

> The real temple is the very Word of God; for to it all humanity must turn, and it is the center of unity for all mankind. It is the collective center, the cause of accord and communion of hearts, the sign of the solidarity of the human race, the source of eternal life.

Peoples of all "races and colors, varying faiths, denominations and conditions" could come together in the House of Worship, "for the ages of darkness have passed away, and the century of light has come. Ignorant prejudices are being dispelled, and the light of unity is shining."

At his talk at Hull House, a community house founded by Jane Addams in 1889 to improve the lives of the poor and working class, 'Abdu'l-Bahá pointed out that ". . . numerous points of partnership and agreement exist between the two races; whereas the one point of distinction is that of color. Shall this, the least of all distinctions, be allowed to separate you as races and individuals?" "God," he continued, "is not pleased with—neither should any reasonable or intelligent man be willing to recognize—inequality in the races because of this distinction."[4]

There was, though, "a power which nothing in the world of mankind can withstand and which will overshadow the effect of all other forces at work in human conditions. That irresistible power is the love of God."[5]

At the Fourth Annual Convention of the NAACP, 'Abdu'l-Bahá began with the biblical statement that human beings were created in the image of God. What did it mean to be "created in the image of God"? 'Abdu'l-Bahá explained that a human being "imbued with divine qualities, who reflects heavenly moralities and perfections, who is the expression of ideal and praiseworthy attributes, is, verily, in the image and likeness of God." The seat of the knowledge of God from where these divine qualities grew was "the heart illumined by the light of God . . . inasmuch as God has endowed man with such favor that he is called the image of God. . ." Therefore, "he who is the image and likeness of God, who is the manifestation of the bestowals of God, is acceptable at the threshold of God—whether his color be white, black or brown; it matters not."[6]

The next day, on a cold and raw day, 'Abdu'l-Bahá laid the cornerstone of what would become the first House of Worship of the continent, the "Mother Temple of the West." He affirmed that the power which had drawn them together was the power of God, the divine favor of Bahá'u'lláh..."[7]

The ground-breaking ceremony for the House of Worship took place during the annual meeting of the Bahá'í Temple Unity. Louis Gregory was one of those in attendance. He gave his first talk to a national audience on this occasion, and the Convention elected him to the Executive Board of Bahá'í Temple Unity, recognizing his great capacity by voting for him unanimously to break a tie. Gregory's life of service now extended across the country.

In the early evening of May 8, 1912, in Washington DC, Agnes Parsons took vases and fresh flowers and chocolate nougat to the apartment[8] in which 'Abdu'l-Bahá would be staying for the next few days and then went on the train station where she and a group of Bahá'ís waited to greet him.[9]

The train ride had been twelve hours long, leaving Pittsburgh at nine in the morning and arriving at Union Station in D.C. at nine at night. So that 'Abdu'l-Bahá could rest, the Bahá'ís who traveled with him pleaded that He allow them to pay for a private cabin for him. He refused their request: "I make certain expenditures only to help people and to serve the Cause of God; and since my childhood I have never liked distinctions."[10]

Despite the long train ride and the late hour, 'Abdu'l-Bahá spoke to the many seekers and well-wishers who sought his presence and his spiritual guidance.[11] To the people assembled at the apartment, He spoke of how people have not been able to recognize the new Manifestation of God because of their literal interpretations of Scriptures. At the Parsons' home afterward, He expounded on economics and the spiritual teachings.

'Abdu'l-Bahá's visit also met with public opposition. Before his talk at the Universalist Church on April 21st, the reverend received a letter of warning about having 'Abdu'l-Bahá speak at the church.[12] The April 25, 1912 edition of the *Washington Post* ran the headline "Persian Priest attracts Women to the Cult of Bahá'ísm." The Hamline Methodist Episcopal Church put a church announcement in the *Evening Star* newspaper on April 27, 1912 about 'Abdu'l-Bahá's talk with the derisive title "Abdu'l-Baha and the Forty Thieves." A minister printed up leaflets attacking 'Abdu'l-Bahá which were distributed in front of the Unitarian Church at one of his appearances.[13]

'Abdu'l-Bahá told the numerous visitors who came to hear him speak at the Parsons' residence on the afternoon of the next day, May 9th,[14] to pay no mind to these public criticisms. Commenting

on the attacks, He said that "The denunciation by the leaders of
religion is a proof of the greatness and influence of the Cause
because no one pays any attention to something insignificant."[15]
The following day, He again assured the Bahá'ís:

> But after I leave, some people may arise in opposition, heaping
> persecutions upon you in their bitterness, and in the newspapers
> there may be articles published against the Cause. Rest ye in the
> assurance of firmness. Be well poised and serene, remembering
> that this is only as the harmless twittering of sparrows and that
> it will soon pass away. If such things do not happen, the fame
> of the Cause will not become widespread, and the summons of
> God will not be heard.[16]

Another large crowd assembled in the residence that evening.
Among them was a man who was bereaved of his brother.[17]
'Abdu'l-Bahá invited him into a private room to speak with him.
Later, he told Mrs. Parsons that 'Abdu'l-Bahá "had said very com-
forting things to him."[18]

The next morning, May 10th,[19] 'Abdu'l-Bahá was brought by
Mrs. Parsons to the offices of the Persian-American Educational
Society. He spoke to the assembled group about the importance
of using consultation in all of their Bahá'í work.[20] On another
occasion, 'Abdu'l-Bahá wrote of consultation:

> . . . take counsel together in such wise that no occasion for
> ill-feeling or discord may arise. This can be attained when ev-
> ery member expresseth with absolute freedom his own opinion
> and setteth forth his argument. Should anyone oppose, he must
> on no account feel hurt for not until matters are fully discussed
> can the right way be revealed. The shining spark of truth com-
> eth forth only after the clash of differing opinions. . . .[21]

'Abdu'l-Bahá then spoke to a group of prominent women about
the rights and education of women. In Chicago, the Master had
promised: "that until woman and man recognize and realize

equality, social and political progress here or anywhere will not be possible."[22]

The movement to extend the right to vote to women in the U.S. was gathering momentum in those days. Much of the general public, though, still saw womanhood as being most naturally fit with creating a home environment that would raise civic-minded citizens. The catastrophe of World War I slowed the voting rights efforts but also demonstrated to the nation the patriotism of the countless women who helped the war effort on the homefront by serving in clerical jobs so men could go fight, working in heavy industry, on assembly lines for factories, manufacturing trucks and munitions, and as railway guards, postal workers, police officers, and fire fighters. For the first time, Black American women were employed by department stores as elevator operators and cafeteria servers.[23]

After his talk to the women, 'Abdu'l-Bahá went with Laura Dreyfus Barney to visit a home for the poor established by her mother, Mrs. Alice Barney.[24] That evening He dined at the Barney home where He spoke to the assembled guests who "floated on a sea of happiness."[25]

The next day, Saturday, May 11th, 'Abdu'l-Bahá left their midst on the train to New York City.

My marriage as you know was entirely brought about by 'Abdu'l-Bahá. I had no thought of marriage when I came to this country.[26]

Louise Mathew[27] wrote these words to Agnes Parsons some years after she attended the groundbreaking ceremony for the House of Worship in 1912. Mathew was an educated British woman who had studied economics, languages, and voice at Cambridge University and continued her vocal training in France, where she became a Bahá'í.

She was on pilgrimage at the same time as Gregory who

remembers them being drawn to each other: "Last year we visited 'Abdu'l-Bahá at Ramleh and the Holy Tomb at Akka and although greatly attracted to each other, not even dimly realized its future bearing."[28] On this pilgrimage, Gregory noted that 'Abdu'l-Bahá described intermarriage between the races as "a good way to efface racial differences."[29]

When they were in the United States, 'Abdu'l-Bahá encouraged Louise by giving her a white rose to give to Gregory. She took this to mean that she should consider Gregory for marriage, and she remembers that "curiously enough after this love began to grow in my heart and the desire for marriage whereas before I only liked Mr. Gregory as a friend." In Chicago, Mathew asked the Master directly if He wished for Louis Gregory and her to be married to which He replied that He did, "I wish the white and the colored people to marry."[30]

Later, 'Abdu'l-Bahá told Gregory that He would be greatly pleased if Gregory and Mathew married. This came as a shock to Gregory. 'Abdu'l-Bahá let him know that marriage was not a requirement but that it would give him much pleasure if such a union was realized.[31]

In the days before the marriage that took place on September 12, 1912, Gregory had written about the need for discretion around their marriage: "But please do not mention this except with the utmost discretion as we do not wish any sensational newspaper articles written at the time and are exerting ourselves to avoid such things."[32]

Gregory's caution reflected the realities of the times in the U.S., not any hesitancy on his part. Marriage between Black and white—any physical relations—were taboo. In most of the United States, it was socially unacceptable for a Black man and a white woman to be in any kind of personal relationship, much less married. Even the appearance of being in one could bring physical harm to the Black man, and accusations of a Black man sexually assaulting a white woman were not uncommon and could quickly result in violence and even lynching.

In that year of 1912, the boxing champion Jack Johnson, a

Black American, married a young white woman. Her mother went to the press accusing him of kidnapping and saying she would rather her daughter spend the rest of her life in an insane asylum rather than marry a Black man. The two left the United States for years. The marriage caused such public outrage that a constitutional amendment was proposed banning intermarriage between the races.[33]

Most of the states—including all those in the South and almost all in the West—had anti-miscegenation laws, and several states made any kind of interracial cohabitation a felony. Several states did away with such laws in the Reconstruction period and many more during the post-WWII decades—though none in the South—but it was only in 1967 with the *Loving v. Virginia* case that went before the Supreme Court, that anti-miscegenation laws were declared unconstitutional. In 1912, the prejudices and attitudes that resulted in such laws were present in daily life, in home after home and town after town and could create real danger for Black Americans, especially for someone like Louis Gregory who had begun what would be a lifetime pattern of travelling throughout the South teaching a new religion.

The small wedding party of only nine people—held not in a church but in a parsonage—had enormous historical and symbolic significance for the people of that time and of the future in the lesson the Master was teaching through it. Gregory describes that important morning:

> Some weeks ago, 'Abdu'l-Bahá, who has watched over Louise and me with the tender solicitude of a loving father, sent me a Message directing me to use the utmost judgment in order to avoid criticism in regard to our approaching Marriage. With me "the utmost judgment" was prayer for Divine Guidance, in which Louise heartily joined me. Our prayers have been heard and answered and we are very happy. Every matter connected with the event went off without friction, although some things were quite difficult.
>
> On last Friday at noon, at the residence of Rev. Everard W.

Daniel, just nine persons were present, including the minister and his wife, the bride and groom. After the ceremony of the Church of England was completed, the groom said, "Verily we are content with the Will of God." And the bride responded, "Verily we are satisfied with the Desire of God". Then Mr. MacNutt read the Tablet of 'Abdu'l-Bahá on marriage. Mr. Braithwaite followed, reading a Tablet revealed to the groom three years ago of which the following is an extract: "I hope that thou mayest become the herald of the kingdom, become the means by which the white and colored people shall close their eyes to racial difference, and behold the reality of humanity." Mrs. Botay closed with the Tablet of Baha'o'llah, *Protection*. The wedding party repaired to the wedding breakfast. In this small company were represented Christians and Jew, Bahá'ís and non-Bahá'ís, the white and colored races, England and America, and the three Bahá'í Assemblies of New York, Philadelphia, and Washington.

During the ceremony, there was a light rainfall. This, Mrs. Nourse says, was a Bahá'í sign, the Bounty of God. After the ceremony the skies cleared, the sun shone and everything a n d everybody seemed happy. The same afternoon we arrived here on our honeymoon. We find ourselves very harmonious and happy.[34]

...the Lord of mankind has caused His holy, divine Manifestations to come into the world. He has revealed His heavenly Books in order to establish spiritual brotherhood and through the power of the Holy Spirit has made it practicable for perfect fraternity to be realized among mankind.[35]

Returning to D.C. after an all-night train ride from Cincinnati, 'Abdu'l-Bahá spoke in the hall of the Universalist Church in Washington on the evening of November 6, 1912, the first day of his third and final visit to Washington, D.C.[36]

Only through the Holy Spirit, He told the audience, can a

universal bond between all peoples be created—all other bonds such as nations, races, families—were limited. Through the Manifestation of God, human beings could be freed from their limitations and "a unity appears which is indissoluble, unchanging and never subject to transformation."[37]

'Abdu'l-Bahá asserted that the "the world of humanity is one and God is equally kind to all." He referenced the war that had just broken out between Balkan states and the Ottoman Empire and violent conflicts between people generally and explained that "the real underlying cause is lack of religious unity and association, for in each of the great religions we find superstition, blind imitation of creeds, and theological formulas adhered to instead of the divine fundamentals . . ." But if we investigate for ourselves and seek to understand the true foundations of religions, ". . . we find them to be one, absolutely changeless and never subject to transformation." The Divine Teachings—common to all religions ". . . instill and awaken the knowledge and love of God, love for humanity, the virtues of the world of mankind, the attributes of the Divine Kingdom, rebirth and resurrection from the kingdom of nature."[38]

Bahá'u'lláh taught that "religion must be the cause of unity and love amongst men" and was "not intended to arouse enmity and hatred nor become the source of tyranny and injustice." If it did, "it would be better to abandon and abolish it." People must be taught the spiritual ways "by kind methods of guidance and teaching to become perfect. Those who are asleep must be awakened. . . . But all this must be accomplished in the spirit of kindness and love and not by strife."[39]

The following day at the Parsons' home,[40] 'Abdu'l-Bahá picked up again on the news of the Balkan War to let the visitors know that Bahá'u'lláh had predicted in his Epistle to the Sultan of the Ottoman Turks that one day his lands would pass out from his hands. These prophecies to the Kings and Rulers a half century ago had been to call them to the new Revelation and bring about peace among nations but this call had gone largely unheeded.

Bahá'u'lláh's purpose had been "to unify mankind, to cause them to agree and become reconciled, thereby manifesting the oneness of the world of humanity, preparing the way for international peace and establishing the foundations of happiness and welfare."[41]

If human beings remained in a state of nature, they would not escape the bonds of nature like the animal. Humanity needs education. The Manifestations of God "... arise to bestow universal moral training." Bahá'u'lláh has come and "flooded the East with light." His teachings have "laid a basis for new institutions which are the very spirit of modernism, the light of the world, the development of the body politic and eternal honor" and His followers, though from diverse backgrounds, have "immediately renounced the spirit of strife and hostility and began to associate in goodwill and fellowship."[42]

The next evening,[43] at the Eighth St. Synagogue, 'Abdu'l-Bahá returned to the theme of the unity of religions. The foundation of religion was that "God is one, the effulgence of God is one, and humanity constitutes the servants of that one God." The essential teachings of religion were the same. The fundamental requirement for human spiritual progress was the "... knowledge of God." Human beings must "... comprehend the oneness of Divinity . . . know and acknowledge the precepts of God and realize for a certainty that the ethical development of humanity is dependent upon religion." Only this way can a human being be in the image and likeness of God. Religion, though, has become a source of conflict "... due to blind imitations of dogmatic beliefs and adherence to ancestral forms of worship."[44] He proceeded to show that Jesus had praised the teaching of Moses, and Muhammad those of Jesus. The essential teachings of all Faiths were the same, only their secondary teachings changed according to the changing times. There was no basis for discord over religion. 'Abdu'l-Bahá finished by pointing out that peace and understanding were the true and only path to God:

Love and fellowship are absolutely needful to win the good

pleasure of God, which is the goal of all human attainment. We must be united. We must love each other. We must ever praise each other. We must bestow commendation upon all people, thus removing the discord and hatred which have caused alienation amongst men. Otherwise, the conditions of the past will continue, praising ourselves and condemning others. . . .[45]

'Abdu'l-Bahá's words challenged the congregation when He spoke about Jewish history and the figure of Jesus Christ. Rabbi Abram Simon may have preferred for Dr. Farid to end the address at that point but 'Abdu'l-Bahá continued. There were parishioners who left during the second part of the address, and there was some restlessness among those who stayed. The rabbi said in his closing remarks that "we are not accustomed to the mention of other prophets than our own, but people of culture all over the world listen to others with ideas different from their own. They may be right, and we may be wrong."[46]

'Abdu'l-Bahá told visitors the next day, November 9th,[47] at the Parsons' residence, that there were people at the synagogue the night before who had been "evidently disturbed" by what He had said and that the rabbi had come to see him earlier. 'Abdu'l-Bahá reviewed with him the points He had made that the Manifestations of God were the Educators of humanity and that they should be judged on how they taught and the effects of their teaching. Through the spread of the teachings of Jesus Christ, the name of Moses had become widespread and Jesus himself had praised the teachings of Moses. What harm was there if the followers of each religion acknowledged the validity of the other? The rabbi agreed with the validity of 'Abdu'l-Bahá's points. Then he asked the Master: "I believe that what you have said is perfectly true, but I must ask one thing of you. Will you not tell the Christians to love us a little more?" To which 'Abdu'l-Bahá replied, "We have advised them and will continue to do so."[48]

That evening, 'Abdu'l-Bahá attended a banquet in his honor given at Rauscher's Ballroom.[49] In the banquet hall, large tables were decorated with flowers and set in the shape of the number

Washington Hebrew Congregation

Rabbi Abram Simon of the Eighth St. Temple

nine. This number has symbolic meaning for Bahá'ís because it is the numerical value in Arabic of the word 'Baha', as in 'Bahá'u'lláh', it's a number of completeness being the highest single digit, and it's the number of the historically known world religions.[50] A calligraphy of the "Greatest Name"—"O Thou the Glory of the Most Glorious!"—in Arabic calligraphy was above

The Eighth St. Temple where 'Abdu'l-Baha spoke

the seat of honor. The guests were in formal attire and greeted the Master with song. Mason Remey stood and on behalf of the Bahá'ís read a prepared statement thanking 'Abdu'l-Bahá and promising him their "obedience and renunciation of the world."[51] 'Abdu'l-Bahá announced to the guests that He would come and serve each of them. He walked around the room giving each person sweets from his own hand and anointing them with attar of rose, creating a real sense of unity among the guests.

'Abdu'l-Bahá invited all of them to ". . . become my partners and coadjutors in servitude." His fervent hope was that ". . . the present meeting may be instrumental in ushering in the day when the standard of the oneness of the world of humanity shall be held aloft in America." He called on everyone to ". . . endeavor with heart and soul to reconcile the religions of the earth, unify the peoples and races and blend the nations in a perfect solidarity."[52]

The following evening, November 19th,[53] 'Abdu'l-Bahá spoke at the home of the Hannens.

As a result of the Hannens' cultivation of friendships with Black America, this meeting—unlike most of those at the Parsons' residence, had a much greater number of Black Americans in attendance.

'Abdu'l-Bahá affirmed that "character is the true criterion of humanity. Anyone who possesses a good character, who has faith in God and is firm, whose actions are good, whose speech is good—that one is accepted at the threshold of God no matter what color he may be." He expressed his joy that "the love of Bahá'u'lláh is in your hearts. Your souls are rejoicing in the glad tidings of Bahá'u'lláh. My hope is that the white and the black will be united in perfect love and fellowship, with complete unity and brotherhood."

Early the next morning, 'Abdu'l-Bahá boarded the train for Baltimore while, "to the amazement of onlookers, they [the Baha'is] gathered around Him, their hearts filled with sorrow and anguish."[54]

'Abdu'l-Bahá had called the Bahá'ís of Washington, D.C. to

work for a universal unity beyond race and religion, to receive the love of God, to attain the knowledge of God, and to follow the teachings of the Manifestation of God. In any gathering where there was the spirit of unity, He would be with them. Now, He was leaving them physically. The rest was up to them.

Notes

1. Morrison, *To Move the World*, 55.
2. 'Abdu'l-Bahá, *The Promulgation of Universal Peace*, 65.
3. Ibid.
4. Ibid. "Talk at Hull House," April 30, 1912 https://www.bahai.org/library/authoritative-texts/abdul-baha/promulgation-universal-peace/-4#067283427.
5. Ibid., 68.
6. 'Ibid., 71.
7. Ibid.
8. The apartment, located at 1340 Harvard St. N.W., Washington, D.C., belonged to the William P. Ripley family. The family temporarily vacated it. 'Abdu'l-Bahá chose this residence for this leg of his trip, but no reason was given in the accounts of the time. (Parsons, *Diary*, 59)

    "The Ripley family would go on to pioneer for the Baha'i Faith to Orlando, Florida later in 1912. Infused with devotion through their close contact with 'Abdu'l-Bahá, the Ripley family remained steadfast despite pioneering alone in Central Florida. Just prior to his passing, Mr. Ripley had three women seekers over for tea who liked to refer to themselves as "We Three." They would go on to form the core of the Orange County Bahá'í Community which continues to this day. The house was built in 1911 selling for $6000, and considered an elegant residence alongside those of Congressmen. In 2006, the house was renovated into the three condominiums it is today" (Mayo, "The Greater Orlando Bahá'í Center.").
9. "Mirza and Mme. Khan, Mr. and Mrs. [Hippolyte] Dreyfus-Barney, Mirza Sohrab, and Mr. and Mrs. Hannen. (Mrs. Dreyfus remained in her motor)." (Parsons, *Diary*, 61)
10. 'Abdu'l-Bahá quoted in Zarqani, *Mahmud's Diary*, 85.
11. There are no official transcripts of the talks 'Abdu'l-Bahá gave during his stay in D.C. during the month of May, 1912 (Authors' note).
12. Ward, *239 Days*, 39.

13. Parsons, *Diary*, 136. According to footnote 15 in the *Diary*, it indicates that this was done outside of the "Unitarian Church when the Mater had spoken there." The last time the Master spoke at the Unitarian (Universalist) Church was on November 6, 1912.

14. That morning, He granted an interview to Mrs. Boyle. In the afternoon, the visitors included "Mrs. W. L. Fisher, Mrs. F. K. Lane, Mrs. Danworth, ex-Justice Henry Billings Brown, Mr. and Mrs. William D. Fonkle, Ms. Gwendolyn, Dr. and Mrs. Gehring, Mrs. Richard Wainwright, Mrs. Leonard Wood . . ." (Parsons, *Diary*, 62; "Fonkle" may be a misspelling):

    Mrs. W.L. Fisher's husband may have been Walter L. Fisher, the Secretary of the Interior under President Taft from 1911 to 1913. He was a member of the Executive Committee of the Chicago Peace Society and an honorary vice president with Jane Addams in 1914 ("Fisher, Walter Lowrie (1862-1935," Jane Adams Digital Edition, https://digital.janeaddams.ramapo.edu/items/show/425.

    Mrs. F. K. Lane (Anne Lane) was married to Franklin K. Lane who served as the Secretary of the Interior from 1913-1920 under President Wilson. He served on the Interstate Commerce Commission on which he made important contributions to commerce law. As Secretary of the Interior, he challenged the laws with respect to Native Peoples by seeing to guarantee equality of status to native Americans and sovereignty for tribal nations. He was an active supporter of the League of Nations ("Franklin Knight Lane").

    Justice Henry Billings Brown was an Associate Justice on the U.S. Supreme Court from 1890-1906. He wrote the majority opinion for the Plessy v. Ferguson that upheld the legality of racial segregation with the principle of "separate but equal." ("Henry Billings Brown")

    Dr. John George Gehring was a neurologist who specialized in treating stress, anxiety, and depression at his clinic in Bethel, Maine, where he saw hundreds of prominent Americans who came for treatment (Andrews, "Dr. John George Gehring").

    Mrs. Leonard Wood (Louisa A. Condit) was married to Gen. Leonard Wood who served as the Chief of Staff of the U.S. Army from 1910 to 1914 and, later, as Governor General of the Philippines from 1921 to 1927 ("Notable Descendants").

15. 'Abdu'l-Bahá quoted in Zarqani, *Mahmud's Diary*, 87.

16. 'Abdu'l-Bahá, *The Promulgation of Universal Peace*, 428-429

17. Joseph Millet; his brother was Frank Millet (Parsons, *Diary*, 63); Francis (Frank as he was called) Millet, was a famous American painter, translator, and one of the founders of the School of the Museum of Fine Arts, Boston, who died when the Titanic sunk on the 15th of April, 1912. This accident was less than a month before John Millet met 'Abdu'l-Bahá.

John was in town to attend memorial services for his brother.

18. Parsons, *Diary*, 63. 'Abdu'l-Bahá also had a private interview with Ms. A. E. Marsland (Ibid., 63). This may refer to Miss Agnes E. Marsland, daughter of George Marsland, the founder of the American Bankers' Association, who was President of the "Order in America," a group seeking esoteric knowledge whose mission was "To form a chair of universal brotherhood based on the purest altruism, without hatred of creed, sect, caste, or colour . . . to study occult sciences of the Orient, and seek by meditation and a special line of conduct to develop these powers which are in man and his environment." Prominent citizens attended their meetings at the Oriental Esoteric Center on Q St. in D.C. They believed a great teacher would be born in the next twenty years who would teach humanity. ("Washington's Most Curious Cult — Under Leadership of a Woman.")

19. According to Parsons (*Diary*, 63), she sent her carriage to pick-up 'Abdu'l-Bahá and then drove to the "Orient-Occident Unity," formerly called the Persian-American Educational Society founded by Ahmad Sohrab. Already there at the office to see 'Abdu'l-Bahá were "Mirza and Mme. Khan and the two older children. Mr. and Mrs. Belmont. Mr. and Mrs. Hannen, Mrs. Struven and others." Mrs. Struven was a Bahá'í who lived in Baltimore with her husband, Howard Struven, who was the first Bahá'í, along with Mason Remey, to circle "for the first time in Bahá'í history, the globe visiting on his way the Hawaiian Islands, Japan, China, India, and Burma" (Shoghi Effendi, *God Passes By*, 261). The Struvens lived at 1800 Bentaloo St. in West Baltimore (Parsons, *Diary*, 155). Also there were Ahmad Sohrab, Dr. Zia Baghdadi, and Dr. Farid (Parsons, *Diary*, 64-65). Among the visitors at the apartment was Mr. Theodore Spicer Simon, a well-known medalist, who was drawing sketches of 'Abdu'l-Bahá who sat a half an hour for him. The authors have chosen Parsons' version for the main text because she was there that morning and wrote her notes that day or the next in a diary whereas Zarqani's notes were written up once he had returned to the Holy Land.

20. Zarqani states that there was a "gathering of distinguished women on the rights and education of women" (*Mahmud's Diary*, 87). Baghdadi also refers to a "Woman's Meeting" ("'Abdu'l-Bahá in America," *Star of the West*, 19). Parsons does not describe a woman's meeting but rather this meeting at the Orient-Occident Unity office (*Diary*, 63).

21. 'Abdu'l-Bahá, *Writings of 'Abdu'l-Bahá*, 87.

22. 'Abdu'l-Bahá, *The Promulgation of Universal Peace*, 77. That afternoon, 'Abdu'l-Bahá was driven by Dr. Farid and Agnes Parsons to the Capitol and 'Abdu'l-Bahá expressed a wish to go inside, where He examined the statuary and paintings, then we walked on the grounds and sat

for a short time near a large tree. We also drove to the [Washington] Monument, and went up to the top in the elevator. Abdul Baha looked with great interest out of each window. I bought a pamphlet, describing the monument, giving pictures and which was sent to Moneer Khanom" (Parsons, *Diary*, 65).

23. March Beamish, *America's Part in the World War*, 259-72.

24. The 4 p.m. group that day included "Dr. Tom Williams, Col. and Mrs. Hopkins, Mrs. Wainwright, Mrs. Lane, Mrs. Hobson, Mrs. Rockwood Hoar, Mrs. Pinchot, Mrs. Richardson, Mrs. Tyson of Baltimore" (Parsons, *Diary*, 65). Mrs. Rockwood Hoar may have been 'Christine Rice' who was the widow of Sen. Rockwood Hoar who passed away in 1906. He was elected to Congress from Worcester, MA, in 1904. She split her time between Washington, D.C. and Massachusetts. In 1915, Rice married Frederick Gillette, the Speaker of the House of Representatives ("Rockwood Hoar Papers").

25. Zarqani, *Mahmud's Diary*, 87.

26. Louisa Mathew in a letter to Agnes Parsons, January 18, 1921, quoted in Morrison, *To Move the World*, 63.

27. Her birth name was Louisa but she was called "Louise."

28. Louis Gregory in a letter to Pauline Hannen, September 19, 1912, quoted in Morrison, *To Move the World*, 64.

29. 'Abdu'l-Bahá quoted in Louis Gregory, *Heavenly Vistas*, Pilgrim's note.

30. Louisa Mathew in a letter to Agnes Parsons, January 18, 1921, quoted in Morrison, *To Move the World*, 66-67.

31. Recollections of Louise Mathew in a letter to Agnes Parsons, January 18, 1921, quoted in ibid., 67.

32. Louis Gregory in a letter to Pauline Hannen, September 19, 1912, quoted in ibid., 67.

33. Stein, "Amendments," 630.

34. Louis Gregory in a letter to Pauline Hannen, September 19, 1912, quoted in Morrison, *To Move the World*, 68.

35. Abdu'l-Bahá, *The Promulgation of Universal Peace*, 391.

36. 'Abdu'l-Bahá arrived at 8:15 in the morning. Agnes Parsons lists herself, Dr. Edward Getsinger, and Ghodsia Khanum, as being there to greet 'Abdu'l-Bahá, Dr. Farid, and Mahmud Zarqani. Ghodsia Khanum was one of the first Iranian women to be educated in the West. She attended the Tarbiyat School for Girls in Tehran, funded in part by Bahá'ís in D.C. Several of the boys and girls attending the Tarbíyat schools received scholarship assistance from the Persian-American Educational Society, a charitable organization formally established in North America in January 1910, because of the efforts of several Iranian and American Bahá'ís. In 1911, she traveled to the United States and addressed the society's inaugural meeting in Washington, D.C. in 1911 ("Ghodsia Ashraf

Khanum").

'Abdu'l-Bahá rented an apartment at 1901 18th St. N.W. where He met visitors and gave talks (*The Promulgation of Universal Peace*, 428). Mrs. Parsons conducted him in her carriage to the apartment. She returned later and found that people had arrived to visit with 'Abdu'l-Bahá. These included Mrs. Helen Hillyer Brown of San Francisco, who was a friend of Mrs. Phoebe Hearst and Ella Goodall Cooper. She was among the earliest Western Bahá'ís to visit 'Abdu'l-Bahá when she was one on the pilgrims who journeyed from the U.S. to see 'Abdu'l-Bahá in March, 1899 ("Ella Goodall Cooper," *Bahá'í World* v. 12, 682). She survived the San Fransisco fire of 1905 though her father's medical office was destroyed. He went on to treat numerous victims of the fire in an empty house, and she published a complete account of the events of that time ("Florence's Family Album: From the Ashes of 1906").

Parsons came at 3 pm, to take 'Abdu'l-Bahá for a "drive" which included going again to the train station, visiting an "ill colored woman," then to see Mrs. John Jay White (Parsons, *Diary*, 128). According to Zarqani (*Mahmud's Diary*, 375-7), 'Abdu'l-Bahá arrives on the afternoon of the November 5th; Zarqani gives an entirely different account of the activities of November 6th. The authors have gone with Parsons' account as she wrote it contemporaneously to the events whereas Zarqani wrote down his memories after returning to Palestine sometime after the events described.

37. 'Abdu'l-Bahá, *The Promulgation of Universal Peace*, 391.
38. Ibid., 394.
39. Ibid., 397.
40. Parsons (*Diary*, 128-129) writes that "this morning 'Abdu'l Bahá made a long visit upon the Turkish Ambassador" and that Sallie Stockton joined 'Abdu'l-Bahá and his Persian assistants for lunch. Stockton was Agnes Stockton Parson's cousin. That afternoon 'Abdu'l-Bahá spoke twice at the Parsons' residence. The first time up in the library with "Mrs. Lane, Mrs. Wilbert, Miss Sigmonds, Rabbi [Abram] Symon, Dr. Williams, Mr. Louden, the Dutch Minister were here, besides the party. General Greely came for a few moments."
41. 'Abdu'l-Bahá, *The Promulgation of Universal Peace*, 399.
42. Ibid., 400-402.
43. According to Parsons (*Diary*, 130-31), 'Abdu'l-Bahá was joined for lunch at her home by General and Mrs. Greely, Mrs. Wainwright, Sallie Stockton, and Dr. Edward Getsinger. Among those in attendance for the afternoon talk (not included in *The Promulgation of Universal Peace*) were Mr. William Carr, Mrs. F.K. Lane, Mrs. Johnston, and Mrs. Fremont Smith, her friend, Herbert Putnam, Mr. H. Butler and others.

Herbert Putnam was the Librarian of Congress. He wrote his impressions of 'Abdu'l-Bahá in a letter to Parsons (Parsons, Diary, 153).

44. 'Abdu'l-Bahá, *The Promulgation of Universal Peace*, 402-410.

45. Ibid, 410.

46. Rabbi Simon of the Eighth St. Synagogue quoted in Parsons, *Diary*, 132. The original congregation was made up of German Jewish immigrants. By 1908, there were three synagogues in the I St. neighborhood. The Washington Hebrew Congregation on 8th St. and I St. was a Reformed congregation known for liberal views and interfaith work ("History"). Rabbi Abram Simon began at the Washington Hebrew Congregation in 1904. A scholar and a community activist, he served in the Red Cross during World War I. In D.C., he served as the President of the D.C. Board of Education and the Conference of Christians and Jews. An elementary school on Mississippi Ave. in S.E. Washington, D.C. was named after him. His broad-mindedness and interest in interfaith may have made him interested in having a visitor as distinguished as 'Abdu'l-Bahá ("A Legacy of Vision"). The reaction of the congregants to 'Abdu'l-Bahá's talk may have been due in part to the fact that the teaching in the synagogue had moved away from literal messianic expectations and many of them were refugees from pogroms for whom hearing about Jesus as the Messiah and Muhammad as a Messenger of God may have been too much.

47. Earlier that day, 'Abdu'l-Bahá went to the Parsons' residence where her son, Jeffrey, was just returning from Dublin, N.H., accompanied by Dr. Stowell. He spoke at 4:30 p.m. to a group in the library and then to another at 8:30 p.m. during which He gave an "informal account" of his conversation with the rabbi (Parsons, *Diary*, 132-133).

48. 'Abdu'l-Bahá, *The Promulgation of Universal Peace*, 411-416.

49. Rauscher's was on the southwest corner of Connecticut Avenue and L Street N.W., D.C. Founded by Charles Rauscher, a French immigrant who became a confectioner and caterer, it had catered high society events for many years and included a large ballroom upstairs (DeFerrari. "How Sweet It Was").

50. Shoghi Effendi to an individual believer, July 9, 1939, *Lights of Guidance*, 415.

51. Zarqani, *Mahmud's Diary*, 381.

52. 'Abdu'l-Bahá, *The Promulgation of Universal Peace*, 428-430.

53. People came in great numbers to see 'Abdu'l-Bahá in the morning such that the apartment's rooms were full. He gave an in-depth talk in the afternoon at the Parsons' residence on Divinity and how to understand God after going for a ride in the carriage,

54. Zarqani, *Mahmud's Diary*, 384.

Chapter 10

The Harder Road

Villiam McAdoo, the Secretary of the Treasury, wrote to
Woodrow Wilson, the newly elected president, in the early
months of Wilson's presidency, that a policy of segregation of federal employees was necessary "to remove the causes of complaint
and irritation where white women have been forced unnecessar-
ily to sit at desks with colored men."[1] Wilson's postmaster general
also expressed to the new President that he found it intolerable
that Blacks and whites should share restroom facilities.

On the campaign trail, Wilson had promised to protect the
advancement of Black Americans: "Should I become President of
the United States, [Negroes] [sic] may count upon me for absolute
fair dealing and for everything by which I could assist in advancing the interests of their race in the United States."[2]

Many Black Americans voted for him, crossing over from the
party of Lincoln to do so. But less than a month after he entered
office, his administration ramped up efforts to segregate the
workforce.

Wilson was a son of the Confederate South. Born in Georgia
in 1856, one of his earliest memories was hearing a passerby
announce in disgust that Lincoln was elected and that war was
imminent. Both of his parents identified completely with the
Confederate cause. Though he became governor of a northern
state and was President of Princeton University, and though as a
president he did try to improve the lot of American workers and
had a vision of international peace and agreement that was ahead

of its time, he retained the attitudes prevalent among whites of the South on which he had been weaned. He once remarked "the only place in the world where nothing has to be explained to me is the South."[3]

He romanticized the Confederate South in his book, *A History of the American People*, which describes the institution of slavery as a kind of "caretaking" arrangement without describing its inherent and pervasive brutality and ignored the treasonous dimensions of secession by emphasizing the proximal cause of secession as a states' rights issue. As the last of the Civil War veterans died out, the idea of a war between morally equal sides became the prevailing historical narrative among white Americans. The Confederacy's loss of the war was a noble but "Lost Cause."

Segregation of the federal workforce had begun under the Theodore Roosevelt administration but was greatly accelerated under Wilson. These were years when there was a renewed assault on the rights of Black Americans. There were vigorous attempts to enforce Jim Crow laws and anti-intermarriage laws in the Northern states, and Black Americans were increasingly excluded from jobs they had traditionally held. Agencies made excuses for not promoting Black Americans, and segregated units were created. Most Black Americans in the Federal government worked for the Treasury, Interior, and Post Office, so it was from those departments that the calls for segregation came.[4]

Before the Wilson administration, about five percent of the Federal workforce was made up of Black employees. They occupied managerial positions, even in some cases heading integrated teams. Wilson's cabinet appointees demoted Black Americans and denied promotions to prevent any from managing white employees. Curtains were installed to separate Black and white office clerks. Sometimes Black employees were made to work in separate rooms. Lockers, lavatories, and lunchrooms were all segregated. In 1914, applicants for positions were required to submit photographs as a way of preventing the hiring of Black employees.[5]

President Woodrow Wilson

Among the worst consequences of these segregation policies was that they deprived Black Americans of access to well-paying jobs that solidified a middle-class status for them and their families and without which, they were much more vulnerable economically. A prominent Black American lawyer remembered how his grandfather was demoted from a supervisor at the Government Printing Office to a messenger at half his previous salary. As a result of the loss of income, he lost his home and died a "broken man."[6]

Wilson did not equate segregation with discrimination. He had the common southern white progressive view of the day that segregation was not a moral issue but a practical way of addressing racial concerns and keeping Black Americans safe.[7] He saw it as a practical matter of expediency:

> I do approve the segregation that is being attempted in several of the departments. . . . I think if you were here on the ground you would see, as I seem to see, that it is distinctly to the advantage of the colored people themselves. . . . I certainly would not myself have approved of it if I had not thought it to their advantage.[8]

During his term as the Governor of New Jersey, Wilson came to be seen as a progressive for his policies, and Black voters who were dissatisfied with the pace of change under Republicans and critical of what they saw as the accommodationist approach to white racism of older Black leaders, supported Wilson's candidacy for President though he was a Democrat. They hoped his progressivism in certain areas would also be applied in advancing and protecting the civil rights of Black Americans. This was a leap of faith on their part because none of the legislation Wilson worked on in New Jersey helped advance the interests of Black citizens.

One Black supporter, who urged Wilson onward in supporting civil rights and who himself presaged the more activist civil rights leaders of the 1950s, was William Trotter, the editor and founder of the *Boston Guardian*, a highly influential paper among Black

Americans. W. E. B. Dubois described the *Guardian* as: ". . . bitter, satirical, and personal; but it was earnest, and it published facts. It attracted wide attention among colored people; it circulated among them all over the country; it was quoted and discussed. I did not wholly agree with the *Guardian*, and indeed only a few Negroes did, but nearly all read it and were influenced by it . . ."[9]

Trotter had corresponded with Wilson and was invited to come to the White House where he sought to get Wilson to stop the advancing segregation in the Federal government:

> *Mr. Monroe Trotter.* Mr. President, we are here to renew our protest against the segregation of colored employees in the departments of our National Government. We [had] appealed to you to undo this race segregation in accord with your duty as President and with your pre-election pledges to colored American voters. We stated that such segregation was a public humiliation and degradation, and entirely unmerited and far-reaching in its injurious effects. . . .
>
> *President Woodrow Wilson.* The white people of the country, as well as I, wish to see the colored people progress, and admire the progress they have already made, and want to see them continue along independent lines. There is, however, a great prejudice against colored people. . . . It will take one hundred years to eradicate this prejudice, and we must deal with it as practical men. Segregation is not humiliating, but a benefit, and ought to be so regarded by you gentlemen. If your organization goes out and tells the colored people of the country that it is a humiliation, they will so regard it, but if you do not tell them so, and regard it rather as a benefit, they will regard it the same. The only harm that will come will be if you cause them to think it is a humiliation.
>
> *Mr. Monroe Trotter.* It is not in accord with the known facts to claim that the segregation was started because of race friction of white and colored [federal] clerks. The indisputable facts of the situation will not permit of the claim that the segregation is due to the friction. It is untenable, in view of the established facts, to maintain that the segregation is simply to avoid race

friction, for the simple reason that for fifty years white and colored clerks have been working together in peace and harmony and friendliness, doing so even through two [President Grover Cleveland] Democratic administrations. Soon after your inauguration began, segregation was drastically introduced in the Treasury and Postal departments by your appointees.

President Woodrow Wilson. If this organization is ever to have another hearing before me it must have another spokesman. Your manner offends me. . . . Your tone, with its background of passion.

Mr. Monroe Trotter. But I have no passion in me, Mr. President, you are entirely mistaken; you misinterpret my earnestness for passion."[10]

President Wilson though, like many white Americans, could not brook an honest conversation about race especially with a Black American who asserted a firm and contrary opinion. Wilson would not meet with him again.

The Bahá'ís of Washington, D.C. had to find a way forward for their community in this society in which racism was the norm and believing in a Faith that taught unity and the abolishment of prejudices of all kinds.[11]

Bahá'ís in D.C. had different understandings of the Bahá'í teachings and how to proceed in terms of integrated meetings. For a small number of white people, the Bahá'í teachings on unity as applied to race were too challenging to the prejudices in which they had been raised. Other Bahá'ís, Black and white, wanted to move ahead and follow the Master's lead and hold integrated meetings. Many whites were somewhere in-between their belief in the Bahá'í teachings expressed by 'Abdu'l-Bahá and their own racial concerns and fear of the condemnation of other white people.

Integrated meetings challenged the racial beliefs of white people. This was especially true for white inquirers who never went into integrated meetings or spaces. To white inquirers, integrated meetings could be a barrier to further investigation of the Faith. Such meetings were, more importantly though, a tangible manifestation of the Bahá'í teaching of unity and a great point of attraction for Black Americans, among whom the Faith had been growing.

In 1914, the Bahá'ís of D.C. decided to give up the hall they were renting as a Bahá'í Center and hold home meetings and rent a hall as needed.[12] This deepened the divisions in the community by not having a common space open to all and allowing people to simply meet as they pleased which reverted to the default racial divisions. One group of white Bahá'ís felt that "mixed meetings" were an obstacle to the growth of the Bahá'í community and wanted to rent segregated and prestigious halls to which they could attract socially prominent white people. Another group saw this as contrary to the Bahá'í teachings and that white inquirers would have to be led gradually to an understanding of oneness. Yet another group thought that a center was unnecessary and that the work of the Faith was that of individuals reaching others through ministering to others and development of one's own spiritual powers.

'Abdu'l-Bahá had taught that Bahá'ís must let go of such differences and deepen their commitment to unity and fellowship and this way, racial differences would fade. This, though, was certainly the harder road. Only by taking the harder road, and doing the more difficult work of meeting together as one community, could racial divisions be lessened, society's ills challenged, and a higher level of unity—visible to the world—be attained. This demonstration of unity was also a significant point of attraction to Black inquirers who could then see a different pattern among Bahá'ís than in the general society.

The Gregorys clearly wanted the Bahá'í community to integrate its activities fully, understanding this to be 'Abdu'l-Bahá's true vision. Their role in the community became "the difficult part of peacemaker, explaining the difficulties of the white people to the colored and the point of view of the colored people to the white."[13]

'Abdu'l-Bahá wrote Joseph Hannen in April 1914, regarding the three meetings:

> O thou who art firm in the Covenant! In the matter of white and colored in Washington great difficulties have arisen amongst the believers. According to what is heard they are divided into two parties and this difficulty will become more intense day by day and may end in strife and contention. Strive ye by all means that this difference may not remain and the believers may become united and agreed. At present, it seems it is nearer to wisdom if a meeting is held specially for the whites, another meeting specially for the colored and a third meeting both for the whites and colored, so that those souls who do not like to associate with the colored race may attend the meeting for the white and those who are out of sympathy with the white may frequent the meeting for the colored and those who are not attached to the colors—white and colored may gather together on a special day or night in one meeting. For the present, this question will not be solved save the quiet execution of this plan, otherwise day by day this difference will increase. In this manner everyone will be untrammeled and will attend any one of the meetings which is to his liking.[14]

In May 1914, a tablet from 'Abdu'l-Bahá was received in which He again addressed this situation:

> I know about everything that is happening in Washington. The sad, sombre news is the difference between the white and the colored people. I have written to Mr. Hannen requesting him, if possible, to arrange a special place of meeting for the white people only, and also a special place of meeting for the colored people, and also one for both the white and the colored, so that all may be free . . . I can see no better solution to this question.[15]

In his use of the adjectives "sad" and "sombre," 'Abdu'l-Bahá reveals his sorrow that racial attitudes were dividing Bahá'ís. He seemed to accept that this is where they were and could only encourage them to strive towards unity and true Bahá'í fellowship. World War I was breaking out, so further communications between him and the Bahá'ís of Washington, D.C. would be difficult.

Unfortunately, there were Bahá'ís who misunderstood 'Abdu'l-Bahá's letter and took it mean that these separate meetings were the preferred arrangement. There were now three meetings of Bahá'ís in D.C. The first was a meeting for white people at the Pythian Temple on Sundays; the Order of the Knights of Pythias was a fraternal order founded during the chaos and divisions of the Civil War to gather men together to do service for society. There was a meeting for Black Americans that was also attended by whites at the Washington Conservatory of music and a 'mixed' gathering at the home of a white Bahá'í.

The meeting at the Pythian Temple drew large audiences but a letter was circulated among the attendees that promoted blatantly racist views that contradicted the teachings of the Faith. Once he read the letter, Joseph Hannen stopped going to the Pythian Temple. He had been asked by 'Abdu'l-Bahá to start a meeting for white people at which he could gradually introduce them to the Bahá'í teaching of the oneness of humanity but the views in the letter were unacceptable, so he began another at Lewis Hall.

The attendance at the Washington Conservatory of Music fell off because it was advertised as the "colored" meeting so Black participants may have been disheartened by the lack of interracial fellowship that had formerly existed on the Wednesday evening meetings. The 'mixed' meeting didn't do well either because the hostess grew concerned about her neighbors and the building management creating problems for her because of the visits to her home by Black Americans. The representatives of the different meetings met together to consult. Joseph Hannen said he would be willing to resume assisting the Pythian meeting but only if the racist contents of the circulated letter were publicly repudiated which the others all unanimously agreed to do.

Louise Gregory wrote about the condition of the community to Agnes Parsons who was now considered the 'mother' of the community:

> I know that you are very anxious to establish harmony among the believers here in Washington and are troubled at the unfortunate state of affairs here that is bringing the Cause into disrepute to the outside world as well as troubling the believers, colored and otherwise. . . .[16]

Louise wrote that she thought 'Abdu'l-Bahá's intention in asking Hannen to have a meeting for whites was so that there could be a private meeting for whites who weren't ready for integrated meetings to learn about the teachings of the Faith and gradually become open to the principle of oneness but that the public meeting should be open to all. To the Gregorys, renting a public hall for a 'whites only' meeting, though, violated the teachings and spirit of the Faith and thwarted its teaching mission:

> Both my husband and myself were exceedingly troubled at the suggestion as we foresaw the disastrous consequences to the teaching [of] the Cause to the colored people, in fact we foresaw all that has happened now—for the work here is practically at a standstill among the colored people and many who were believers or on the brink of becoming so will have nothing to do with us.[17]

Agnes Parsons cared very much for the spiritual health and well-being as well as the advancement of the Bahá'í community of Washington, D.C. She doubted though, that the intentions of 'Abdu'l-Bahá were as the Gregorys and the Hannens understood them:

> . . . we hear such murmurs as the following: "Although 'Abdu'l-Bahá allows this, it is well understood what he really wishes." "Although the Pythian Temple Meeting for white people alone

is established, it will surely exist but for a short time, when it will be changed into a mixed meeting." In this way the undercurrent of dissatisfaction continues, causing the members of that meeting to feel unsure of their ground. Also, those who are not in sympathy with it are restless, hoping for change. Dear Friends! I hope you will try to develop a sympathy for every kind of meeting which is for the spread of the Cause, for 'Abdu'l-Bahá has called such meetings "good."

A Universal Teaching must have a message for all. Those who object to mixed meetings must find a prepared way to receive the Message in the manner they are willing to take it. It is for us to provide the means.

Undoubtedly there is an important work to be done by the believers whose special field is the Pythian Temple. They should work spiritually and quietly, making every effort to overcome the prejudice of the inquirers. If this work be done wisely, before the minds of the opposers are fully awakened to the fact that belief in the Oneness of Mankind is spreading among the people, it will have had the necessary time to become so rooted in the hearts that nothing can dislodge it. This belief is a new and tender flower of this Blessed Day, and if we should force it into the strong winds of opposition, too soon, its precious growth will be retarded. However, we should know that the ideal Bahá'í meeting is the mixed meeting, and all should be united in giving to it the love and sympathy essential to success.[18]

The people in Parsons' world to whom she might introduce the Faith no doubt would have objected strongly to attending interracial meetings thus her concern focused on a gradual approach to teaching white people whose racial attitudes she well knew. Clearly, she was committed to and concerned with the growth of the Bahá'í Cause in general and shepherding the community wisely. She herself, though, was not involved in the teaching of Black Americans as the Gregorys and the Hannens were, and she did not take into consideration—or she may not have even been aware of—the perspective of Black Americans. Their perspective was not one that she had to consider in her daily life. So the issue of the racist letter circulated at the Pythian meeting did not come up for her, and she may have been wholly unaware or did not fully appreciate the meaning of the drop-off in attendance of Black Americans.

Though certainly a devoted follower of the Bahá'í Faith and of 'Abdu'l-Bahá, Parsons had difficulty shaking the prejudices with which she was raised. Interracial marriage, for example, gave her serious concern despite 'Abdu'l-Bahá having encouraged it. She wrote to Alfred Lunt, a white Bahá'í in Boston who was active in the administration of the Bahá'í community, to ask about the legal aspects of intermarriage. She was concerned that Bahá'ís would be breaking the law. He wrote back to her that twenty-five states and the District of Columbia did not recognize or did not allow racial intermarriage. He gave an accurate and wise assessment of the situation among the Bahá'ís:

> The superstitious and limited biological ideas taught today will vanish before the flame of the Love of God, and the problem [intermarriage], simplified, will become merely what it should be, an individual problem of selection. But this cannot be unless we bravely and unfalteringly herald the *Principle*. In Washington, as you know, some of the souls are in an attitude of apology and distortion toward the great principle elucidated by Abdu'l-Baha [the oneness of mankind]—seeking to please and attract the believers in superstition on this subject. Had the Manifestations Themselves adopted this policy of concealment and compromise, they might have preserved thereby their lives and possessions, but the Divine Civilization would never be realized. Baha'o'llah said that the Divine Laws are revealed strictly according to the *capacity* of the people at the time of Appearance. The unanswerable corollary must be that had the people of the world not been capable today of living according to the law of *oneness* it would not have been decreed.[19]

Coralie Franklin Cook, who was deeply involved in teaching the Faith to Black Americans, took up her pen during these

Coralie Franklin Cook, renowned suffragist, elocution teacher at Howard University and long-serving member of the DC Board of Education, and Director of the Home for Colored Children and Aged Women.

years to write her thoughts to 'Abdu'l-Bahá. She addressed him as "Honored and dearly beloved Teacher," then admitted that "Writing a letter to you is like no other writing. No sooner do I take up the pen with that intention than I seem somehow, to be ushered into your very Presence."

She went on to give her candid assessment of race in the U.S.;[20] this was soon after Wilson's inaugural:

> Race relationship, in the Southern States especially, but more or less thru out the country is in a deplorable condition. In many instances where friendship, mutual sympathy, and good will ought to exist, hostility and venom are manifested by the whites and are met by distrust and dislike on the part of the colored people. To cite the contributing causes which had led up to this direful situation—culminating recently in acts of certain public officials, leading toward segregation and discrimination among the employees of the federal government itself—would be to write a book. Chief among them however it is safe to say is the popular delusion called "social equality." By some strange phenomenon certain white people think or affect to think, that if a colored person shares in the ordinary privileges which pertain to comfort and convenience, or political or civil right that it means "social equality"—that is to say, if permitted to vote, to take part in civic festivities or parades, to ride in the same car, to attend the same public school or place of worship or to be buried in the same grave yard means "social equality." To any but a morbid or diseased mind this seems like unbelievable absurdity which, practically carried out, is making the position of the colored people almost unbearable and robbing the American white people of any rightful claim to an exalted position among the nations of men, because they are either active participants in, or silent witnesses of the gross injustice. And yet, as in the days of slavery, when certain heroics rose up against the iniquities of that awful system and said, "These things must not and shall not be," so now the maligned and persecuted black man is not without friends.

She then appraised the attitudes towards inter-racial marriages:

> No phase of the color question excites so much rancor and misrepresentation as the one of mixed marriage. It is constantly made use of all classes of whites from the Statesmen to the boot-black and now includes some so-called Bahá'ís to arouse

passion and strife and to flatter Saxon vanity. If the whole truth were told, it must be said that many colored people are as strongly opposed to inter-racial marriage as the whites who rant and tear continuously, the difference being that colored people entertain no fear of whole-sale absorption as some whites apparently do.

She summarized the progress made by Black Americans since emancipation by dint of their own efforts and yet, "Instead of this marvelous achievement appealing to all that is best and noblest in whites it has seemed to have a contrary effect." Laws and courts made every effort to thwart Black progress. When Black Americans looked to "the followers of Christ for protection and championship . . . one by one they have given into the mandates of the Race Problem or Prejudice. . . ."

She then articulates the perspective which Parsons didn't understand or may not have fully appreciated that for the Black person:

> The Bahá'í Cause is his "last hope" but that if "he be asked to face a line of cleavage in it, his faith will be broken and not only HIS faith but the faith of all those white persons who believe in Divine teachings, worse than all to discriminate would be to furnish the enemies of the Negro with new weapons both of offence and defiance for would they not say, "See, we are right! Even the Bahá'ís could not hold out."

She cautioned those Bahá'ís who did not believe the principle of racial unity should be implemented fully at that time and to wait for a better time:

> To any one of the Bahá'í faith to whom the tempter says "temporize" or let the matter work itself out, I say beware! When was ever a mighty Principle championed by temporizing or delay? I know some must suffer both white and black, but who better able to wear the mantle of suffering than the real Bahá'í?

The blessed Báb, Bahá'u'lláh, and the Center of the Covenant, have blazed the path for our feet to tread. Dare we turn back? If anyone has come to realize his duty to the community in which he lives, to the country to which that community is a part, to the world to which the country must contribute its share in the making of the world's Progress and to His God, must not embrace the Teachings of Bahá'u'lláh as the Greatest instrument put in the hands of man for bringing all the nations of the earth under conscious harmony with the Will of God?"

By moving through tests, she believed, the Bahá'í Cause could fulfill its greater promise:

Every noble principle, every lofty ideal, every rule of conduct in the Bahá'í Faith can be defended by passages of our own Bible, the Faith is seeking followers at a time when it would seem as if the Universe itself were challenged to choose between Peace and War, brotherhood and disunion, right and wrong. It is not plain to all that the TEST is crucial and that the times are so momentous that what may seem for the present to hold back the Cause of Bahá'í may be in reality the one thing that will put world progress forward immeasurably.

By the 1910s, the last of the Civil War veterans were dying out and with it, the remaining first-hand witnesses of the horrors of the conflict that tore the nation apart. A reimagining of the Confederate Cause as a noble but 'Lost Cause', took root in the imagination of many white Americans, especially Southerners. The Lost Cause ideology depicted the Confederate leaders and soldiers as being the ones fighting for freedom, blamed the Union as the aggressors, and negated the great suffering of Black people under slavery with its violence and dehumanization, and erased the memory of the role of Southern whites in this exploitation. In the decades after the Civil War, Confederate memorials and civic

Associations were founded that incorporated this ideology, planting it firmly in the public square of civic discourse and later—in the form of statues—in the literal public squares.

This ideology became a way for white Americans to resolve the Civil War by elevating the conflict into a romantic realm:

> The Lost Cause became an integral part of national reconciliation by dint of sheer sentimentalism, by political argument, and by recurrent celebrations and rituals. For most white Southerners, the Lost Cause evolved into a language of vindication and renewal, as well as an array of practices and public monuments through which they could solidify both their Southern pride and their Americanness. In the 1890s, Confederate memories no longer dwelled as much on mourning or explaining defeat; they offered a set of conservative traditions by which the entire country could gird itself against racial, political, and industrial disorder.[21]

The Lost Cause ideology helped to alleviate the feelings of dishonor among white Southerners and became generally accepted among white Americans by the 1900s as a means of national reconciliation, but this reconciliation was at the expense of the social and economic progress of Black Americans.

This ideological narrative of the Civil War and the Reconstruction was depicted on the silver screen in one of the most groundbreaking—in terms of the art and technology of movie-making—movies in the history of early American film: *The Birth of a Nation*. D. W. Griffith, a filmmaker who co-founded United Artists company and developed the idea of financing for full-length movies, directed this three-hour silent movie—the longest ever made—using groundbreaking techniques of close-ups, fade-outs, and recreating seemingly large-scale battle scenes. The plot, characterizations, and themes all reflect the Lost Cause narrative: plantation life as an ideal in which Black servants were content and secure under benevolent masters; free Blacks as unable to handle freedom and drinking and attacking others

without any respect for law and order; Reconstruction as a disaster for 'true whites' of the South—its embodiments in the film is an abolitionist Northerner depicted as physically deformed and limping and lusting after a mixed-race woman, and the politician overseeing Reconstruction in the state is a mixed-race man who lusts uncontrollably after women. These characterizations were at the racial heart of this ideology and were the ones that Black Americans fought very hard to change. At the end of the film, the saviors of the South appear—the Knights of the Ku Klux Klan who ride into town and save the day.

When the movie came out, the NAACP and many Black Americans attempted to counter its effects by boycotting it and having cinema owners delete especially egregious scenes. None of these efforts deterred white Americans from going to see it in large numbers. It went on to become a blockbuster. *The Birth of a Nation* was the first movie to be screened in the White House when President Wilson viewed it in February 1915. Soon after the release, the Knights of the Ku Klux Klan were reactivated as an organization. By 1925, the organization had grown and been accepted to the point where 25,000 members paraded in full robes down Pennsylvania past the White House.

"'Abdu'l-Bahá has made it all possible."[22]

So wrote Louis Gregory to Joseph Hannen during his 1916 teaching trip. 'Abdu'l-Bahá had issued "a trumpet call to action" to American Bahá'ís.[23] On small postcards sent from Palestine that came through the mail that had to travel across the chaos of World War I, 'Abdu'l-Bahá's words urged the Bahá'ís in the United States and Canada to teach the Cause.

These "Tablets of the Divine Plan," the first five of which were published a month before Gregory left for his trip, gave the Washington, D.C. Bahá'ís a much-needed infusion of spiritual energy by challenging them with a mission. Their beloved 'Abdu'l-Bahá called the Bahá'ís "O ye heralds of the Kingdom of God" and praised the efforts of the Bahá'ís in the Southern States. He then noted that there were few believers in those states and instructed them to ". . . either go yourselves or send a number of blessed souls to those states, so that they may guide the people to the Kingdom of Heaven." He assured them that "if a person become the cause of the illumination of one soul, it is better than a boundless treasury."[24]

Louis Gregory responded. He undoubtedly saw this as his

sacred calling and told the Bahá'í Temple Unity Board that he felt "his pilgrimage should be in the South."[25]

Gregory was an experienced travelling speaker. Only the year before, in the summer of 1915, he had gone to Nashville and Atlanta. In Atlanta, he got to see the teaching work of Fred Mortensen, a young white man who had once ridden the rails a long distance to meet 'Abdu'l-Bahá. Mortensen taught the Faith in Atlanta to two prominent Black clergymen, Bishop Flipper and Dr. Ponton who then proclaimed the Faith actively themselves. In Atlanta, Gregory became the close companion of another white Bahá'í, James Elmore Hays: "We went everywhere together, eating at the colored Y.M.C.A. He said he was badly scared when he received news of my coming but afterward revived his courage."[26] Hays was presented at Gregory's numerous talks in Atlanta showing a living example of interracial cooperation.

While on his teaching trip in 1916, he described to Joseph Hannen a dream he'd had:

'Abdu'l-Bahá was standing before an audience in the attitude of teaching. By his direction I was serving as a waiter, passing to the people bread from a tray. When the wafers reached the people, they were transformed into tablets and upon them they were to indicate how many of them accepted the teachings and became Bahá'ís. An overwhelming number of those who received the tablets thus signified by writing their acceptance. I awoke feeling very happy."[27]

Over the course of the six-week speaking trip, Gregory estimated that he spoke to some 15,000 people, mostly students at colleges. Despite the long hours in sub-standard Jim Crow train cars and coal dust and eating poor food, he returned to D.C. "very happy over the journey, which gave wonderful opportunities and privileges for service..."[28]

Filled with zeal and aware of the lack of Bahá'ís and Bahá'í institutions in the South, he felt compelled to do more. He and Louise decided to sell their house, and he sold his newly opened real estate firm and declined an offer to teach at the Howard University Law School. The funds these sales made available enabled him to continue with his speaking tours. Louise supported him fully but did not travel with him through the South as this would have been much too dangerous. She endured loneliness as her offering to the Cause.

He was "grateful to God that through Divine Favor the way is opened to this unworthy servant." Now he would "be able to spend the best part of the year in the field."[29] In October of the following year, 1917, he began another trip, a pattern that would span the next fifteen years.

Louis Gregory lived now in imitation of the Master. Making do with little but the necessities, he rose at dawn to pray and spoke to whomever and wherever he was asked. In Louisville, Kentucky, he gave talks at the New Thought Center, Methodist, Congregational, and Baptist churches, a state university, women's groups, a socialist group, and a socialist church, as well as engaged in numerous small group and individual conversations.

Gregory's vision was never narrowed to one group or set of opinions. He dialogued—as 'Abdu'l-Bahá had—with Black and white, progressive and conservative, educated and uneducated, all denominations, all political leanings. While always seeking to increase understanding between Black and white Americans and promote the advancement of Black Americans in society, Gregory was always willing to speak about any of the teachings of the Faith to open the hearts and reach waiting souls. Sharing the message of the Faith gave him spiritual energy.

Thanks to his efforts and those of many others in the wake of the Tablets of the Divine Plan, the new Teachings were proclaimed to many. One of those who hearkened to the Message was Dr. Alaine Locke, one of the great minds in the country. He was the first Black American Rhodes Scholar and came to be seen as the intellectual father of the unfolding Harlem Renaissance, a great outpouring of Black American art, literature, music, dance, and thought, that sought to give a deeper and more realistic expression of the Black experience. Raised in a broad-minded and educated family some of whose members had lived in other countries, Locke had a universal outlook in matters of culture and faith so the universal ideals in the Bahá'í teachings spoke to him.

In the same year, 1918, that Locke became affiliated with the Bahá'í Faith, a son, Amoz, was born to the Gibsons, a Bahá'í family in Washington, D.C. The father, William Gibson, had been a minister but after attending a Bahá'í meeting at which Harlan Ober spoke, he and his wife, Deborah, soon became Bahá'ís. Amoz and his wife, Mary, served the Faith in Mexico and on Navajo land where many native peoples became Bahá'ís. He served the Faith in many capacities locally and nationally until he was elected the Universal House of Justice in 1963, becoming the first Black American to serve on that Institution.[30]

World War I came to an end in 1918. Over 350,000 Black American men served in the "Great War" that devastated Europe. Black combat units were formed, and hundreds of Black officers were trained. Black Americans demanded that their men be allowed to form combat units that would see action fighting for the country. White labor boards in the South were also eager to conscript landowning Black men. Black draftees and officer trainees were usually treated with great disrespect at training facilities, with Black officers often not being saluted by white soldiers.

Black service units performed vital and extremely dangerous functions on the battlefield such as digging trenches removing unexploded shells, clearing barbed wire and disabled equipment, and burying soldiers killed in action.

Two major combat Black divisions, the 92nd and 93rd, took the field in Europe. White officers spread false rumors about the 92nd which damaged their reputation. By contrast, their French counterparts who fought with the Division in the Marbache region decorated its members for their bravery. The 93rd fought in France alongside French soldiers and were so tenacious and effective in fighting the Germans that they were nicknamed the "Harlem Hellfighters." Its members were the first Americans to be awarded the French Croix de Guerre for valor in combat.[31]

On the 11th of November, 1918, the armistice was declared, and the long and bloody War was over. The victorious soldiers returned home. But for the Black American veterans, instead of being honored and celebrated by the American public, they were subject to widespread mob violence in what became known as the "Red Summer" of 1919.

In Washington, D.C., a young white woman claimed that she had been harassed by two Black men. Her husband was a naval employee, and the story made the rounds of sailors on a weekend holiday. By word of mouth and lurid, inaccurate headlines, the story grew far larger and included the rumor that gangs of Black Americans were roaming the streets terrorizing people. Over a hundred drunken servicemen went into the Black neighborhood of Bloodfield brandishing pipes, clubs, and pistols, and began beating Black citizens as they came upon them. For four days, Black citizens were indiscriminately beaten and knifed, including one right in front of the White House. Black soldiers set up blockades to protect Black property such as Howard University and defended homes wherever they could using the weapons they had. President Wilson took no action for several days before sending the troops. In D.C., some forty people were killed, and it took 2,000 troops to restore order.[32]

Similar violence erupted in Chicago, Charleston, and Cleveland and in twenty-five small towns. In Arkansas, two hundred and fifty-seven sharecroppers were murdered in two days. Across the country seventy-eight men were lynched and eleven Black men were burned alive.[33]

This sudden surge in white racist violence erupted at that time because of a confluence of causes, each aggravating the other. Many whites feared the return of Black men who'd served as soldiers and who might not resume their subservient status. The

A Black home in Chicago destroyed by white rioters during the
Red Summer of 1919.

economy had gone into a downturn, increasing the competition over jobs, especially in cities to which Blacks were migrating from the South. Lurid and inaccurate headlines in newspapers spread false stories and fed rumors. Stories of the outbreak of the Russian Revolution in 1917 stoked fears about the rise and spread of communism. Leadership in the U.S. government failed to calm public fears, counter the violence, and protect Black citizens.

World War I was a broken promise to Black Americans, especially to those who had served. Risking their lives to make the world safer for democracy had not made them safe at home, improved their prospects, lowered barriers to advancement, elicited the admiration of white citizens, or resulted in being honored for their valor and heroism. But they had seen a world outside of the United States. They'd had the experience of fighting and from the Red Summer on, Black Americans became much more publicly assertive in defending and pursuing their constitutional rights.

From April 26 to May 1, 1919, hundreds of Bahá'ís gathered at the Hotel McAlpin in New York City for the 11th National Bahá'í Convention—called by 'Abdu'l-Bahá the "Convention of the Covenant."[34] After twenty million deaths and twenty-one million wounded, the guns in Europe had gone silent, and a Peace Conference in Paris set the terms of the victors. Contact with 'Abdu'l-Bahá could now be fully renewed.

The Tablets of the Divine Plan were formally introduced and unveiled by region in public ceremonies on each day of the Convention. There were Tablets written to the Northeastern States, Southern States, Central States, Western States, and Canada and Greenland. 'Abdu'l-Bahá was lighting the path for American Bahá'ís:

> O THOU kind Lord! Praise be unto Thee that Thou hast shown us the highway of guidance, opened the doors of the kingdom and manifested Thyself through the Sun of Reality.[35]

Their mission was to take the new message to all parts of the country and the world:

> The moment this divine Message is carried forward by the American believers from the shores of America and is propagated through the continents of Europe, of Asia, of Africa and of Australasia, and as far as the islands of the Pacific, this community will find itself securely established upon the throne of an everlasting dominion.[36]

To fulfill this mission, they would have to allow the Divine Spirit to move through them to others unimpeded by self. Whoever arose would be aided by Grace:

> O my God! O my God! Thou seest me in my lowliness and weakness, occupied with the greatest undertaking, determined to raise Thy word among the masses and to spread Thy teachings among Thy peoples. How can I succeed unless Thou assist me with the breath of the Holy Spirit, help me to triumph by the hosts of Thy glorious kingdom, and shower upon me Thy confirmations, which alone can change a gnat into an eagle, a drop of water into rivers and seas, and an atom into lights and suns? O my Lord! Assist me with Thy triumphant and effective might, so that my tongue may utter Thy praises and attributes among all people and my soul overflow with the wine of Thy love and knowledge.[37]

Beginning with the publishing of the first five in 1916, the Tablets of the Divine Plan released a great spiritual force. Hundreds inquired about the Faith in St. Louis. New communities were founded in Springfield, Massachusetts, and Hartford and New Haven, Connecticut. More than twenty people were part of the Harlem, New York, Bahá'í community, after much teaching there. Martha Root, a journalist, boarded a boat for South America in July, for the first of her many world journeys, to spread the new message. Fanny Knobloch, Pauline Hannen's sister, moved to Germany. Women sowed the seeds of the Faith throughout the world.

After the Convention, Louis Gregory began a speaking trip through the South with the goal of going to all sixteen states listed in the Tablets to the Southern States. This time, an administrative support system manned by Joseph Hannen and others to keep track of places visited, interested persons and other information relevant to founding new Bahá'í communities was set up. For many legs of this trip, Gregory was joined by Roy Williams, a Black American who had become a Bahá'í in Harlem. Williams traveled widely throughout the South and proclaimed the Faith to many, following up with Gregory's contacts when they traveled separately. 'Abdu'l-Bahá referred to him as Gregory's "fellow-traveler," a title which William felt honored to be called.[38]

It was not possible to do much if any advance planning for the stops they made so Gregory and Williams had to be resourceful, not to mention courageous, as they were proclaiming a new Message in a devoutly religious region of the country and, as Black men travelling through the South and in towns where in some cases, they knew no one. Often, Williams and Gregory met with the police ahead of any public meetings and let the authorities know who they were and what their intentions were to preempt potential problems.[39] They did not allow the racial violence of 1919 to stop them and saw the teaching of the new message as a healing balm.

The doors opened. At Clark Atlanta University, Williams was ordered off the stage by the University President for speaking of Bahá'u'lláh and Jesus as equals but then the faculty invited him to finish his talk with them privately. Another time, he spoke to over one hundred ministers at a single gathering after which the Bishop commanded them to open their pulpits to him. At the Holiness Church in Dallas, Texas, the pastor's objections were overridden, and Gregory spoke to five hundred parishioners. He arrived at 3 p.m. in Corsicana, Texas, and by evening had found a room for lodging and a friend who would open her house for a meeting. Gregory phoned ten people of whom six came and were moved enough to order literature to start their own study class.[40]

Memphis, Tennessee, became a hub of Bahá'í activity because of George Henderson, well-known in the community for the business college he had founded, who taught the Faith to all who would listen. By the time of Gregory's visit there in 1917, there were fifty-seven Black Bahá'ís and three white. Integrating the Bahá'í meeting would prove challenging because the white Bahá'ís, though undoubtedly sincere in their Faith, were conditioned by the Jim Crow environment and the consequences for themselves if they were seen participating in integrated gatherings.[41] Doris McKay, a white Bahá'í, spoke with a group of white believers in 1921 about the importance of integrating the meetings:

> . . . the Feast [is] an inclusive community meeting. It is through this institution that we demonstrate the oneness of mankind to a skeptical world made up of warring nations. It is through the Feast that we prove that we are not just one more selective society, but a unit truly composed of diverse elements which have learned to function together. In its spirit, the 'breaking of bread' together, with a feeling of love and fellowship, becomes a sacrament, something which would represent the appearance of the New Day in our Southern states.[42]

She got through to two of them:

> Then I went around and asked each member, one by one, for an expression of feeling. Clara Keller and Johanna Zimmerman were the first to respond. "If we're going to call ourselves Bahá'ís, then let us BE Bahá'ís."[43]

Memphis continued to struggle with the pressures of Jim Crow but an integrated community did emerge and an integrated Assembly was elected in 1941 with George Henderson as one of its members. Henderson was one of three of the main teachers of the Faith in the South along with Harriett Gibbs Marshall who was originally from Arkansas and Caroline W. Harris who taught the Faith in Harper's Ferry, West Virginia. These three and a group of Black travelling teachers, though small in number, proclaimed the Faith to a large number of Black Southerners.[44]

Teaching the Faith among Southern whites was much harder going for Bahá'í travelling teachers. The Jim Crow laws and deeply held segregationist beliefs proved very hard to overcome in building integrated communities. In Louisville, Gregory was welcomed into the home of a wealthy white woman who was a new Bahá'í and held integrated feasts. But when Ellen Beecher, a white Bahá'í travelling teacher, came to Louisville to have a Bahá'í Assembly elected, she found the new Bahá'í felt she could no longer hold integrated meetings: "she considered it would be fatal to the Cause to bring the two races together, and again, it would ruin her reputation and influence in this City—she would simply be ostracized."[45]

Gregory may well have felt discouraged at times by the obstacles presented by the prejudices of whites but thought that the answer was to do more proclamation of the Faith among them: "They [the white Southerners] are perhaps more orthodox [than Blacks] and will not so readily open their established institutions, but there is a vast work for teachers among them."[46]

Though the attitudes persisted to varying degrees in white Bahá'ís, there were those who showed great courage when it came to race. Roy Williams remembered the young white Bahá'í, James Elmore Hays in Atlanta, as being "entirely devoid of any racial prejudice" who would come "under cover of darkness walking across the city sometimes very late at night, he would come to our house at 2 Beckwith Street and sit, eat and talk for hours—just a happy intimate fellowship."[47]

Dr. James Charles Oakshette was an Englishman who worked at the *Atlanta Constitution*. Williams remembers that he met Oakshette and that, "During my first teaching trip I met Dr. Oakshette by arrangement with him in his office in the Hurt Building. This had to be done very secretively but he never showed any fear. . . Of all the Southern or Northern Bahá'ís I have met all over the country I can truthfully say that . . . Dr. Oakshette

personified the best ideals of the cause under all conditions—
even the worst that existed in Atlanta around 1919-1920 trip."⁴⁸

Among the most courageous of the white Bahá'ís and one
who was a key figure in organizing the teaching of the Faith in
the South was Joseph Hannen whom Louis Gregory referred to
as "Brother Joseph." One of his duties for Gregory was to pick up
and forward the mail to him and Williams while on their trips.
In a letter at that time, Gregory wrote to "Brother Joseph" and
mentioned how much he was looking forward to seeing the mail
when he got to Shreveport, Louisiana. But on January 27, 1920,
Hannen picked up the mail to be sent on and as he was crossing
the street, he was fatally struck by a car. The letters destined for
Gregory had his blood spatter on them, "a symbolic testimony of
his last service to the friends."⁴⁹

Notes

1. Gordon Davis, "Wilson, Princeton, and Race."
2. Woodrow Wilson, quoted in Nancy J. Weiss, "The Negro and the New Freedom: Fighting Wilsonian Segregation" *Political Science Quarterly* 84 (1969): 63.
3. Saladin Ambar, "Woodrow Wilson."
4. Rudwick Meier, "The Rise of Segregation," 178-179.
5. Richard Rothstein, "On renaming the Woodrow Wilson School." In 1907 Louis Gregory and a judge went to eat lunch at the D.C. City Hall lunchroom and were denied service despite being members of the bar. *The Washington Bee* (9 March, 1907) wrote: "Ex-Justice of the Peace E.M. Hewletter and Attorney Louis G. Gregory entered the lunchroom in the City Hall Wednesday afternoon and asked to be served. This room is set apart for members of the bar only, but it is frequented by white persons who are not members of the bar, but whenever a colored member of the bar enters this particular dining room objections are made. . . . The waiter informed them that they could be served. Mr. Hewlett was then visited by the proprietress of the lunchroom and she asked him his name. He informed her, and was about to hand his card when she said, "O! I don't want it; I thought it was you." Mr. Hewlett demanded to be served, but the proprietress was obdurate and said that she would not. She was informed that he would report her to the marshal, who would remove her from the building, as he did the former proprietor of the dining room for a similar offense. She said she didn't care. . . . To prevent the outside public from using the dining room, a notice is placed over the door which reads as follows "For members of the bar . . . . it seems that it applies to the white members of the bar only, because the colored public, and all colored employees in and around the Court House and City Hall occupy the lunch counter, where they sit upon high chairs like animals at a trough."
6. Rothstein, "On renaming the Woodrow Wilson School."
7. Lunardini, "William Monroe Trotter's Meetings," 252, f. 10.
8. Wilson in a letter to H. A. Bridgman, editor of the *Congregationalist and the Christian World*, September 8, 1913, quoted in Lunardini, "William Monroe Trotter's Meetings," 252, f. 10.
9. Dubois, *Dusk of Dawn*, 37.
10. *The Crisis*, January, 1915, 119–20, quoted in Katz, *Eyewitness: The Negro in American History*, 389–90.
11. The material in this section is from Morrison, *To Move the World*, chapter 8.
12. Studio Hall at 1219 Connecticut Ave.
13. Louis Gregory, quoted in Morrison, *To Move the World*, 73.

14. 'Abdu'l-Bahá, Tablet to Joseph Hannen, 21 April, 1914, US Bahá'í National Archives, Tablets of 'Abdu'l-Bahá Collection.

15. 'Abdu'l-Bahá in a letter to Edna Belmont, 1 May, 1914, Bahá'í National Center, quoted in Morrison, *To Move the World*, 75-76. Historical document.

16. Louise Gregory in a letter to Agnes Parsons, 21 December, 1914, quoted in ibid., 77.

17. Louise Gregory in a letter to Agnes Parsons, 21 December, 1914, quoted in ibid., 78.

18. Agnes Parsons to the "Washington Friends," 13 October, 1915, quoted in Morrison, To Move the World, 78-79.

19. Alfred Lunt to Agnes Parsons, 4 April, 1914, quoted in ibid., 65.

20. The following selections from Coralie Franklin Cook come from Etter-Lewis and Thomas, *Lights*, 237-243.

21. Blight, *Race and Reunion*, 266.

22. Louis Gregory in a letter to Joseph Hannen, quoted in Morrison, *To Move the World*, 85.

23. The first five Tablets of the Divine Plan were published in *Star of the West* on September 8, 1916.

24. 'Abdu'l-Bahá, *Tablets of the Divine Plan*, 12.

25. William H. Randall in a letter to Agnes Parsons, October 2, 1916, quoted in Morrison, *To Move the World*, 84.

26. Louis Gregory quoted in ibid., 83.

27. Louis Gregory in a letter to Joseph Hannen, quoted in ibid., 85.

28. Louis Gregory quoted in ibid., 85.

29. Louis Gregory in a letter to Alfred Lunt, 23 September, 1917, quoted in ibid., 86.

30. Francis, "Amoz Everett Gibson."

31. Bryan, "Fighting for respect."

32. Higgins, "Red Summer of 1919."

33. Sauer, "One Hundred Years Ago."

34. The Convention was then called the "Mashrekol-Azkar Convention and Bahá'í Congress," as one of its purposes was the continued effort to build the Bahá'í House of Worship, the "Mashrekol-Azkar."

35. 'Abdu'l-Baha, *Tablets of the Divine Plan*, https://www.bahai.org/library/authoritative-texts/abdul-baha/tablets-divine-plan/tablets-divine-plan.xhtml?dbfcbo9b.

36. Ibid., 40.

37. Ibid., 72-73.

38. 'Abdu'l-Bahá in a letter to Louis Gregory July 24, 1919, quote in Morrison, *To Move the World*, 103.

39. Janet Ruhe-Schoen, *Champions of Oneness*, 156.

40. Morrison, *To Move the World*, 103. On Gregory's teaching trip in 1921, Minister I. E. Lowery in Columbia, South Carolina, blamed Gregory's teaching for harming a young Black man's mind and warned against the Bahá'í Faith: "But when we heard Dr. Haygood say that 'Professor Gregory of Washington, D.C., will say a word,' then our treacherous memory by association recalled the fact that about 15 years ago, when we were stationed at Old Bethel in Charleston, a man by that same name came to that city and delivered several lectures on the Bahá'í religion in some of the churches and halls. At that time there was a brilliant young lawyer in Charleston who was a member of Old Bethel. ...This young lawyer was christened in this church and grew up in the Sunday School, became a member and a trustee of this church. This young lawyer took hold of the new religion and tried to master it...until he completely lost his mind and had to be brought to the insane asylum here in Columbia. ...We heard Professor Gregory at Sydney Park on the fifth Sunday afternoon in Columbia, and can truly say for him that he was really eloquent and forceful. ... The principles seem to be all right, but the Lord Jesus Christ is not recognized in them, and any religion that has no Christ in it, is not worthy of the attention of intelligent Christian people. And any attempt to teach, enforce and build up a religion without Christ will be an utter failure. The Bahá'í religion teaches love, but it is not the love that Christ taught ... Nicodemus, a ruler of the Jews, was a man who believed in, and taught the Bahá'í religion, but Christ told him that he must be born again. And no man can love God and his neighbor without being converted.

But another word concerning the young lawyer who was brought to the asylum. After he was brought here his parents wrote us to visit him as often as possible and we did so. The first time we called to see him he held in his hand a little pamphlet, and we asked him for it .... we found it to be a book on the Bahá'í religion. We took it from him and brought it home, knowing that it was this that caused him to lose his mind. He eventually died in the asylum. ... But while this young man embraced the Bahá'í religion, he never left his church, and his body was taken back to the church of his parents and to the church of his childhood, and from this church he was buried. This is what the Bahá'í religion did for a brilliant young lawyer.

Professor Gregory spoke several times in Columbia and each time was shrewd enough to conceal his real purpose ... But while the people admired his oratory, they failed to accept his teaching. The impression he seemed to have made was short lived, and soon passed away. But there may be a few who like the young lawyer referred to above, who will follow the professor." ("Rev. L. E. Lowery's Column").

41. Morrison, *To Move the World*, 104.

42. McKay quoted in Buck, "Despite Jim Crow."

43. Ibid.

44. Morrison, *To Move the World*, 105.

45. Letter of Ellen Beecher to Alfred Lunt, 7 April, 1921, quoted in ibid., 107.

46. Louis Gregory quoted in ibid.

47. Roy Williams quoted in ibid., 108.

48. Morrison, *To Move the World*, 108-09.

49. Charles Mason Remey quoted in ibid., 110.

Chapter 11

"The Convention for Amity Between the Colored and White Races Based on Heavenly Teachings"

The public race amity work with which the American Bahá'í community became closely identified began formally with 'Abdu'l-Bahá. Louis Gregory remembered:

> It was following His return to the Holy Land, however, and after the world war that 'Abdu'l-Bahá set in motion a plan that was to bring the races together, attract the attention of the country, enlist the aid of famous and influential people and have a far reaching effect upon the destiny of the nation itself. This was the first convention for amity between the races and He placed its responsibility entirely in the hands of one of his most devoted American followers, Mrs. Agnes S. Parsons, whom He lovingly called His daughter.[1]

Agnes Parsons went on pilgrimage to 'Abdu'l-Bahá in the Holy Land in early 1920. She was completely devoted to 'Abdu'l-Bahá and the Faith. The D.C. Bahá'í community looked up to her because of her high social position and her sincere devotion, and though generous and thoughtful towards others, she ventured little outside of her social circle and its conventions. Then one evening on this pilgrimage, she was caught completely off guard:

> One evening at supper time when there were about twenty, twenty-two or twenty-four people at the table. 'Abdu'l-Bahá suddenly turned to me, quite out of the blue ... and said: "I want you to arrange a convention in Washington for amity between

the colored and the white." I thought I would like to go through the floor, because I did not feel I could do it.[2]

She and the Master exchanged a few more words and then, "a very extraordinary thing happened. I felt suddenly the power of his creative words. . . ."[3] In selecting her for this important task, 'Abdu'l-Bahá was putting the responsibility for taking the initiative of the race amity work on a white person, thereby making an important statement about the importance of practicing the Bahá'í teachings even when they were difficult. Americans lived in a Jim Crow system that benefitted white citizens, so Bahá'ís from this background were going to have to make a sustained and proactive effort to go beyond the system and build friendships with Black Americans. Only in so doing could real Bahá'í communities be created and the Divine Remedy applied to the nation.

Returning to America, Parsons now had to organize a major event—something she had never done. That event was about racial unity, an issue about which she had always been ambivalent on some level. When she turned to her society friends, they were indifferent. Nothing was materializing. Then her friend Ms. Louise Boyle, a Bahá'í of Washington, D.C., had her meet former Senator Moses B. Clapp who had Black American friends. Parsons spoke at some length with him during which time he recommended she adopt an approach that would not be politically polarizing but, rather, positive in its approach. Parsons decided that the event should "lift the whole matter up into the spiritual realm and work for the creation of sentiment." Parsons felt that Clapp was the "instrument whom 'Abdu'l-Bahá used to give me the plan."[4]

Louis Gregory attended gatherings on the "race issue" that had focused on lessening the barriers of discrimination. He wrote to Parsons regarding the conference that while this was good, "Nothing short of a change of hearts will do. Unless the speakers are able to make the power of love felt, the occasion will lose its chief value." He wanted people to work towards unity which he believed could only be done with the spirit of the Faith guiding the conference:

There are many, many souls throughout the South today who are working and longing for a better day. But without the Light of Abha [Bahá'u'lláh] their efforts seem infantile and helpless. Even some members of the state inter-racial committee, earnest, thoughtful, hard-working men, have voiced to me despair. If the Washington inter-racial congress is along these conventional lines I fear it will like the others, be fruitless. But if it be aflame with the Fire of Divine Love, the hearts will be powerfully influenced and the effect will be great in all the years to come.[5]

To organize the conference, Parsons gathered four of her capable female friends: Mariam Haney, Louise Boyle, Gabrielle Pelham,[6] and Martha Root. They began their work in 1921 only a year and a half after the worst racial violence in recent memory, so they were surprised to find that their efforts met with much goodwill. Gregory wrote that "the workers had unusual experiences and the spirit of reconciliation seemed to sweep the city."[7] The committee distributed nineteen thousand programs to institutions and businesses throughout the city. Martha Root did all the publicity. [8]

With help from her friends, Parsons wrote a direct, thoughtful, and all-encompassing mission statement of purpose that reflected her Bahá'í beliefs:

Half a century ago in America slavery was abolished.

Now there has arisen need [sic] for another great effort in order that prejudice may be overcome.

Correction of the present wrong requires no army, for the field of action is the hearts of our citizens. The instrument to be used is kindness, the ammunition—understanding. The actors in this engagement for right are all the inhabitants of these United States.

The great work we have to do and for which this convention is called is the establishment of amity between the white and the colored people of our land.

When we have put our own house in order, then we may be trusted to carry the message of universal peace to all mankind.[9]

Gregory saw the purpose of the conference as being "race understanding," but he also hoped "to convey the Bahá'í teachings to the nation's capital and many interests centered there and radiating therefrom."[10] To ensure a Bahá'í perspective and spirit throughout the program, the organizers asked a Bahá'í to chair each session.[11]

The conference—formerly known as The Convention for Amity Between the Colored and White Races Based on Heavenly Teachings—opened on Thursday evening, May 19, 1921. The session was chaired by William H. Randall, a Bahá'í from Boston who was the president of a shipping company and who had become a Bahá'í after several encounters with 'Abdu'l-Bahá. He opened by explaining to the audience:

> This convention is not called for the purpose of discussing racial differences. We all realize that we are living in a remarkable day—perhaps a new day. To me its great expression is a call to the human family that war must cease: that races and nations may come together in a new spirit.
>
> If evolution means anything, it means that these great ideals must become a fact; that is, the bringing together of the white and colored races. Sixty years ago, the public realized the necessity of abolishing slavery and in that way solved a great problem. Lately, the public is trying to solve the problem of political freedom, and the solution is near. The thing now is the coming together of all races.
>
> The only problem before us is love, tolerance, and sacrifice. We must live as a nation in peace and we must live as a people in peace.[12]

Dr. Jason Noble Pierce, pastor of this Congregational Church where this conference was being held and which had a history of supporting the advancement of Black Americans, gave the opening invocation in which he called upon God to help people realize that all are one, each one his brother's keeper. Then a Bahá'í hymn was sung: "... Great day of one religion / When all are understood

/ One faith in Life Eternal / One God, One Brotherhood."[13]

The first presenter of the conference was Sen. Samuel M. Shortridge, a senator from California and supporter of Prohibition, who spoke on "The Relation of the Times to World-Wide Peace":[14]

> How can we become one people? It is done by doing justice to all men, whatever colors, of whatever degree or whatever status in life. Peace has come to the nation but I want peace among our people. War called upon many of our sons and daughters to make sacrifices. I shall never forget that the colored man of the country gladly marched to death that their country, my country, might live. I shall never forget that in every war in which the country has engaged that colored fought and died for their country, and I say without any desire or purpose of arousing a dissenting thought. I shall never forget that colored men died for the Republic which enslaved them. I always have announced that in all proper waysthat I would be their champion and friend. . . .[15]

The senator was followed by Albert Vail who spoke on "The Radiant Century of the Passing of Prejudice." Vail, a former Unitarian Minister with a doctorate of Divinity from Harvard University, began his association with the Bahá'í Faith after meeting 'Abdu'l-Bahá. He asserted that, "Nobody knows the trouble prejudice has brought to the world except the loving heart of God, who is today leading His children to unity and obedience."[16]

Vail chaired the Friday 20th morning session, opening it with a prayer for America revealed by 'Abdu'l-Bahá. Theodore Burton, a senator and then congressman from Ohio, spoke on "The New Co-operation":

> The races must dwell in amity in this country because they live side by side. The colored race should be recognized by white men, not only because the Constitution of the United States requires it but by the Divine power of God. Both races must

learn to understand each other. If a crime was committed by a colored man his people should help in bringing him to justice. At the same time, if a crime was committed and the offender unknown, and a colored man happened to be around, people should not jump to the conclusion that a colored man committed it.

We are to take an important place among the nations of the world, but we must first put our own house in order. One of the most serious blots on our national life is that of lynching. This is not against the colored man alone, but against the white as well. I am ready to do whatever can be done, by constitutional amendment or otherwise, to remove this frightful blemish from the nation.[17]

Charles Lee Cook from Louisville, Kentucky, followed. Despite having been wheelchair-bound his entire life and been discouraged by his parents to pursue his interests, he became a brilliant and highly successful inventor who designed and made devices for steam engines. He gave a substantial percentage of his money away. Broad-minded in his outlook, he hoped this convention would be one step towards achieving universal human brotherhood:

The world is looking to this country for social justice. There is great work ahead in bringing about racial understanding. All must face it and help to achieve it, and not bury their heads in the sands of optimism. Individuals must do their part in this great work. Let's try to vindicate the divinely appointed mission of America. Break every bond of misunderstanding."[18]

Cook finished his presentation with a tribute to 'Abdu'l-Bahá.[19] Louis Gregory then began his talk on "The New Springtime," by expressing appreciation to the whites who had fought for the freedom of slaves and the advancement of Black Americans. As he later wrote, "... praise of the good in man is in reality praise of God, since all good comes from the one Source."[20] He then proclaimed the arrival of the Bahá'í teachings and their universality:

> The divine springtime has appeared and the great enlightened
> principles, which are the light and progress of the whole world
> of humanity, are set in motion. These relate to the most great
> peace, the universality of truth, to the great law that humanity
> is one, even as God is one, to the elevation of the station of
> woman, who must no longer be confined to a limited life but
> be everywhere recognized as the equal and helpmeet of man.
> These pertain to the universality of education, to the oneness
> of language, to the solution of this economic problem which
> has vexed the greatest minds of the world and its noblest hearts
> and to that supreme dynamic power, the Holy Spirit of God,
> whose outpouring upon the whole world of flesh will make this
> a world of light, joy, and triumph.[21]

Dr. Alain Locke chaired the Friday evening session and praised
the conference for striving to be one in heart and mind in the
pursuit of mutual support and understanding which exemplified
the new spirit of this day. The first speaker was Rep. Martin B.
Hadden, a longtime congressman from Chicago, Illinois, where
the Faith had been established for some years. He asserted that:

> In a democracy all citizens must be treated on a basis of exact
> equality. Laws must be made impartially and executed without
> discrimination for any reason. Since their liberation the colored
> people have made wonderful progress, reducing their illiteracy
> to only 20 percent and accumulating a vast amount of property.
> Peonage and lynching must not be permitted. The government
> should uphold its own dignity by enforcing justice.[22]

Next, Mr. Alfred H. Martin, the head of the D.C. chapter of the
Ethical Culture Society, a secular religion that focused on an
agreed set of values by which people lived but without theological creeds or rituals and that was oriented towards public service.
Martin spoke on "The New Internationalism and Its Spiritual

Factors," and about race, he said:

> This problem can be solved only by rising to the spiritual conception of democracy. According to this conception the more efficient should help the less efficient. It is for the whites of the North and the South to uplift the backward blacks, with no presuppositions of unfitness or inability to gain the prizes of citizenship for those who prove themselves capable; and the blacks in turn must serve as missionaries to those whites who are so victimized by prejudice that they cannot see the potentialities behind the dark skin.[23]

Saturday morning began with the reading of the Bahá'í "Unity Prayer": "O God! O God! Unite the hearts of Thy servants and reveal to them Thy great purpose..." M. Mountfort Mills,[24] a lawyer in New York City who was taught to pray by 'Abdu'l-Bahá, chaired the morning session and opened by outlining a Bahá'í vision of the future: "We are forwarding a more farreaching purpose than is indicated by the program alone. We seek that mighty Force to develop a new civilization. Amity between the races is a by product of this. This civilization requires intelligence of the heart."[25]

He then read a message for the conference from 'Abdu'l-Bahá:

> Say to this convention that never since the beginning of time has a convocation of more importance been held. This convention stands for the oneness of humanity. It will become the cause of the removal of hostilities between the races. It will become the cause of the enlightenment of America. It will, if wisely managed and continued, check the deadly struggle between these races, which otherwise will inevitably break out.[26]

William Randall spoke first that morning about how "A New Pathway of Universal Peace" went through the door of the human heart:

> If we let these ideals so beautifully expressed come down into

the heart they will be a glorious reality. The door of the heart of humanity has been opened and we find love and love. My note is the power of God. We live too much in the past. This is a new age. Let us live according to its ideals. Severance, service and selflessness are the three Graces of the new day. God gives us these as a banner of peace to the world of humanity. God is looking down upon this convention. His spirit sees in you the universal reality. The real king is the law of God. However much we love democracy, let us not forget the sovereignty of God. Our true freedom is allegiance to this sovereignty. As we give ourselves to it we enter the age of spiritual citizenship for the whole world. This is what Christ meant when He told men to pray that the Kingdom of Heaven might become visible upon earth.[27]

Martha Root then came forward to read messages from officials, including one from Lt. Gen. Nelson A. Miles, one of the last surviving Civil War generals, whose message expressed his support for the cause of the conference.[28] This was followed by Ahmad Sohrab who spoke on "Bible Prophecies of Universal Brotherhood."

Howard MacNutt chaired the Saturday afternoon session and opened with a reading from the Bahá'í Writings: "O Children of Men! Do you know why We have created ye from the same dust? That none shall glorify himself over the other..."

Coralie Franklin Cook then gave a presentation on "Colored Poets and Their Poetry." She was the only female speaker at the conference—women giving public talks was still a rarity in those days. She discussed the poetry of Phyllis Wheatley, who was born in West Africa before being sold into slavery and then bought as a servant girl for Mrs. Wheatley of Boston. Her first name, Phyllis, was that of the slave ship that brought her from West Africa, and her last name was that of her owners. The Wheatleys took the very unusual step of giving her an education. She proved a talented student and read Greek and Latin by the time she was a teenager. She eventually became a well-known published author and was emancipated. In her talk, Cook also touched on the work of Paul Lawrence Dunbar, a nationally known Black author. He wrote some of his most well-loved verses in a form of Black American pre-Civil War dialect and wrote the lyrics to the first Black American musical to be mounted on Broadway, *In Dahomey*. Another writer Cook included was Jean Fauset, who wrote fiction during the coming decade that gave an honest and positive depiction of Black middle-class life, part of a new realism that was a facet of the literature of the Harlem Renaissance, instead of the Jim Crow stereotypes that were prevalent in popular culture.

After a musical interlude and by popular request, Charles Lee Cook came to the front to speak a second time. He emphasized the value and importance of faith, trust, and mutual assistance between the races by telling the story of the Black youth he had mentored and who had now found professional success. He praised all those present as "noble souls who have come to lay the cornerstone of a great reality!"[29]

The last speaker of the conference was Fazel Mazandarani, a Persian Bahá'í scholar whom 'Abdu'l-Bahá had sent that year to the United States and Canada to teach the new Faith.[30] He spoke on "The Solution to the Race Problem in the Orient."

> The aims of all the Prophets of God, while they underwent persecution, was the establishment of peace among the people of the world. . . . However, there has always been a ray of light through the gloom of tyranny and injustice. The law of progress is due to this. Now again it is in our midst.[31]

He then spoke about the religious and ethnic conflicts in Persia which were deep and the appearance of "a great spiritual movement":

> The Divine Bounty rained down and thousands of people were filled with the power of God. The Divine Love brought a community of interest . . . Liberal ideas were introduced among the children in schools. The children being simple and coming from

Fazel Mazandarani (front row wearing white turban) at a Baha'i gathering in
Washington, D.C. Agnes Parsons (front row 2nd from right).

God without prejudices, grew up knowing God and His Laws. In
reality, children enter the world without any fanaticism, but are
taught these things by their elders. . . . We must put aside narrow
and limited notions, for we see the harm they have done others.
It is now the age of Divine justice and universal service.

Mazandarani ended his talk—and this first Race Amity
Conference—with these words:

The Sun of Reality has dawned from the horizon of the world
. . . The banner of Universal Peace will be hoisted! Gloom will be
dispelled. We shall be as the leaves of one tree and the flowers
of one rose-garden, and all the friends of God will embrace each
other.[32]

The participants lingered a long time after those words basking in
the fellowship and speaking together about possible next plans.
The hall had been full for each session and overflowing with
such good will that people were filled with hope. M. F. Harris, an
audience member, remembered:

I attended every session, day and night . . . Many times throughout the meetings I did with much effort restrain my tears. My
heart leaped and throbbed and many times almost burst within
my breast. I am a colored man . . . My race as a whole, I believe,
is quite ready to welcome the glad day when all will be brothers.
. . . The trouble is nearly unilateral. God give us the day.[33]

This conference bringing together Black and white marked an important step in the spiritual growth of the Bahá'ís of Washington,
D.C. who had struggled to become racially integrated. The spirit
of 'Abdu'l-Bahá gave Bahá'ís the courage and motivation to put
into practice the Bahá'í teachings and stand for racial amity.

Agnes Parsons was lifted beyond what she thought she could
do. She trusted in the wisdom of 'Abdu'l-Bahá. She allowed her
faith to transform her and, in so doing, she gained a deeper understanding of unity. 'Abdu'l-Bahá wrote to her that year: "It is
the spirit of oneness which imparts new life to the hearts of the
people of the world." The Master knew she genuinely believed
in the new message: "Really thou art a true Bahá'í and the fire of
the love of God is in fervor in thy heart. Therefore thou art the
cause of the promulgation of the Teachings of God and strivest
after harmony between the white and the colored." 'Abdu'l-Bahá
praised her efforts in the promotion of racial amity:

> The formation of the Congress for the colored and the white
> is productive of eternal glory for thee and is conducive to the
> comfort and ease of the continent of America, because if the
> colored and the white do not acquire harmony between them,
> there will appear great difficulties in the future."[34]

This conference set off a pattern of interracial work by the
American Bahá'í community that continued for decades to come.
Racial Amity conferences were held that decade in Springfield,
Massachusetts; New York, New York; Philadelphia, Pennsylvania;
Dayton, Ohio; the Green Acre Bahá'í property in Eliot, Maine;
Chicago, Illinois; Montreal, Canada; Urbana, Illinois; Wilmette,

Illinois; Rochester, New York; Boston, Massachusetts; Detroit, Michigan; Atlantic City, New Jersey; Pittsburgh, Pennsylvania; and Cincinnati, Ohio; and in addition, smaller race amity events in other cities.[35] But the one organized by Agnes Parsons and her friends was the first and, as 'Abdu'l-Bahá explained:

> . . . was like the Mother, from which in near future many other meetings shall be born. But thou wert the founder of this Convention. The importance of every principle is at the beginning, and the first person to raise the banner of the unity of the white and the colored, wert thou.[36]

In the Holy Land later that year, 1921, 'Abdu'l-Bahá related two dreams to his family members. In the first:

> "I seemed," He said, "to be standing within a great mosque, in the inmost shrine, facing the Qiblih, in the place of the Imám himself. I became aware that a large number of people were flocking into the mosque. More and yet more crowded in, taking their places in rows behind Me, until there was a vast multitude. As I stood I raised loudly the call to prayer. Suddenly the thought came to Me to go forth from the mosque. When I found Myself outside I said within Myself: 'For what reason came I forth, not having led the prayer? But it matters not; now that I have uttered the Call to prayer, the vast multitude will of themselves chant the prayer.'"[37]

Those around him knew how far He had travelled to raise the call of the new day—from Palestine to Egypt to Europe to North America and back.

He related a second dream after He walked in from the garden in the back of which was a room He had been sleeping in: "I dreamed a dream and behold the Blessed Beauty, (Bahá'u'lláh) came and said unto me, 'Destroy this room!'"[38]

On Friday, November 25th, 'Abdu'l-Bahá went to the mosque for the noon-day prayer. Poor people gathered around outside to wait for him. Coming out, He gave each one a coin.

Later that afternoon, He walked in his garden with an elderly believer. Pointing out the flowering garden, He said:

> Behold, what the spirit of devotion is able to achieve! This flourishing place was, a few years ago, but a heap of stones, and now it is verdant with foliage and flowers. My desire is that after I am gone the loved ones may all arise to serve the Divine Cause and, please God, so it shall be. Ere long men will arise who shall bring life to the world.[39]

He had a fever on Saturday, but it broke enough on Sunday that He could receive local officials to whom He spoke and gave gifts. He told all the Bahá'ís to go to the Tomb of the Báb and celebrate a feast of the Covenant, the day of celebration He had set aside for the believers instead of an observance of his physical birthday. The host of the feast was disappointed that He could not join them, but the Master said later: "But I was there, though my body was absent, my spirit was there in your midst. I was present with the friends at the Tomb. The friends must not attach any importance to the absence of my body."[40]

On Sunday night, the daughters of 'Abdu'l-Bahá stayed with him in his room to watch over him. He woke around one in the morning saying He was too warm. His daughter approached, and He asked her to raise the net around the bed as He needed more air. She brought him water, which He drank, and then a little food. He asked her: "You wish me to take some food, and I am going?"

Over at the house where the pilgrims were staying, there was a loud bang on the door. Fujita, 'Abdu'l-Bahá's gardener, lit a candle and opened the door to see who was there. The doctor in the pilgrim group was needed. Several of the pilgrims made their way to the Master's house and went into his room where they saw two doctors, one the ladies of 'Abdu'l Baha's family sitting on the edge of the bed, and his daughter kneeling next to it. 'Abdu'l-Bahá

Star of the West

The funeral procession of 'Abdu'l-Bahá, Tuesday, November 29, 1921

was lying in the bed with his eyes closed. The doctors said there was nothing further to do. His daughter and one of the pilgrims readjusted the pillows under 'Abdu'l-Bahá but He was absolutely still. More pilgrims and guests filtered into the room. Quiet weeping began. A sheet was laid over 'Abdu'l-Bahá's body. The lamentations grew loud. Each person came forward to kiss the place where 'Abdu'l-Bahá's feet were resting.

In England, Shoghi Effendi, 'Abdu'l-Bahá's grandson, received a phone call to come to London to the office where mail for Bahá'ís in England was distributed. The young man was studying at Oxford University and working hard to master the English language so that he would be prepared when the day came for him to return to Haifa and serve his beloved grandfather, possibly as a secretary and translator. When he walked into the office, he found that no one was in there for the moment but he saw a telegram with 'Abdu'l-Bahá's name. It read: "His

Holiness 'Abdu'l-Bahá ascended Abhá Kingdom. Inform friends. Greatest Holy Leaf."[41]

Shoghi Effendi collapsed. For several days, the English Bahá'ís had to watch over him and care for him. He was able to rouse himself despite his intense grief and the overwhelming and disorienting sense of loss and make his way back to Haifa.

There, in the Master's House, he received a second blow almost as incomprehensible as the first. 'Abdu'l-Bahá had left a will in an envelope addressed to Shoghi Effendi in which He described his grandson as "the blest and sacred bough" whose shade "shadoweth all mankind," that he was "the sign of God, the chosen branch, the Guardian of the Cause of God." Shoghi Effendi, twenty-four-years-old and with no foreknowledge of this whatsoever, was now the Head of the Bahá'í Faith, to whom all the Bahá'ís would turn for guidance on all matters large and small, in whose hands all its administrative affairs would now rest, and whose interpretations of the Bahá'í Writings would carry the weight of absolute authority.

In the person of Shoghi Effendi and the station conferred on him by 'Abdu'l-Bahá in his Will and Testament, the covenant that began with Bahá'u'lláh remained unbroken. The unity of the Bahá'í community was preserved. Bahá'ís had a source of authority to which they could look to for guidance in all spiritual matters, direction in their teaching and administrative work, and succor during challenging times.

In the years after the first race amity conference in Washington, D.C., Parsons continued to be actively involved in the race amity work through its ups and downs. Despite continuing to be challenged by her conservative tendencies, she persisted and was obedient to Bahá'í institutions who urged her on in this service. She and Gregory remained sincere friends, with Parsons even seeking his advice on personal matters, and Gregory holding her in high esteem.

There was a lull in race amity activity in part due to the shock of 'Abdu'l-Bahá's passing. Gregory continued to be involved in organizing and speaking at the conferences as well as doing public outreach to like-minded organizations. The Bahá'í efforts were unique in that they were purposely interfaith.[42]

The Gregorys moved to Springfield, Massachusetts, and much to Louis Gregory's concern, the race amity work in D.C. slowed down considerably. Gregory was concerned about the racial tensions in the city but many Bahá'ís of D.C., left on their own, remained ambivalent about this kind of work.

Louis Gregory continued to champion the cause of race amity, speaking publicly and writing to individuals and Bahá'í institutions. He was appointed to the National Assembly Bahá'í Committee on race amity. Agnes Parsons was its chairperson and he, its executive secretary. Gregory was asked to concentrate on the work of the committee rather than continue his travel speaking tours so for eight years, he worked to put the race amity efforts on a firm foundation. Parsons, as chairperson, continued to be cautious in her approach to race amity work while Gregory had a leavening effect on the members.[43]

Race amity also had an important champion: Shoghi Effendi. He wrote to the committee:

> . . . the future growth and prestige of the Cause are bound to
> be influenced to a very considerable degree by the manner in
> which the adherents of the Bahá'í Faith carry out, first among
> themselves and in their relations with their fellow-men, those
> high standards of inter-racial amity so widely proclaimed and
> so fearlessly exemplified to the American people by our Master
> 'Abdu'l-Bahá.[44]

The spiritual transformation of the individual would cleanse the heart of prejudice:

> I cannot believe that those whose hearts have been touched by
> the regenerating influence of God's creative Faith in this day will

find it difficult to cleanse their souls from every lingering trace of racial animosity so subversive to the Faith they profess."[45]

The change in white people was essential to Black Americans accepting the Faith and beyond: "Shoghi Effendi says that the tranquility of all the peoples of the earth depends on this one thing, the coming together of the White and the Black."[46]

Shoghi Effendi's letters on this subject helped Agnes Parsons to see that spiritual equality meant social equality as well, a tangible evidence of equality in the workings of society and daily life. She grew in her understanding and continued her race amity work.

Gregory wrote a letter of appreciation to her: "Shoghi Effendi appears greatly pleased with the work of the committee of which you are the chairman . . . your splendid cooperation at all times and your deep and sacrificial interest in this particular line of service."[47]

Shoghi Effendi expressed his respect and appreciation to Gregory:

> . . . I have nothing but admiration and gratitude for the heroic constancy, mature wisdom, tireless energy, and shining love with which you are conducting your ever-expanding work of service to the Cause of Bahá'u'lláh. You hardly realize what a help you are to me in my arduous work. Your grateful brother, Shoghi.[48]

Notes

1. Louis Gregory, "Racial Amity in America: A Historical Overview," 655.
2. Agnes Parsons quoted in Morrison, *To Move the World*, 136.
3. Parsons quoted in ibid., 136.
4. Parsons quoted in ibid., 137.
5. Gregory quoted in ibid., 138.
6. Pelham was one of the "best known musicians in the City" among Black Americans. She was on the Board of the Washington Conservatory of Music on which Harriett Marshall Gibbs served as well ("Washington Conservatory of Music"). She was the first woman to be awarded a bachelor's degree in music at Adrian College (Michigan) and the first Black American to hold a formal teaching position in Michigan State's Music Teacher Association (Boyd, *Black Detroit*, 75). She belonged to the Delta Sigma Theta sorority, which included Coralie Franklin Cook (*The Mirror*, 84).
7. Gregory, "Racial Amity," 655.
8. Morrison, *To Move the World*, 139. The conference was held at the Congregational Church at 10th and G St. NW, Washington, D.C., from May 19-21, 1921.
9. Buck, "The Bahá'í 'Race Amity' Movement," 13.
10. Gregory, "Racial Amity," 655.
11. Morrison, *To Move the World*, 139.
12. William H. Randall, quoted in "Amity of races," *Evening Star*, 2.
13. Gregory, "Convention for Amity," 117.
14. On the official program, this slot was a talk by Rep. Moses B. Clapp but Gregory's report on the conference has Senator Shortridge here. The title of the talk on the program has been used here.
15. Senator Samuel M. Shortridge quoted in "Amity of races," *Evening Star*, 2.
16. Albert Vail quoted in Gregory, "Convention for Amity," 117.
17. Congressman Theodore Burton, quoted in "Amity of races," *Evening Star*, 2. Note: "From 1882-1968, 4,743 lynchings occurred in the United States. Of these people that were lynched 3,446 were Black. The Blacks lynched accounted for 72.7% of the people lynched. These numbers seem large, but it is known that not all the lynchings were ever recorded. Out of the 4,743 people lynched only 1,297 white people were lynched. That is only 27.3%. Many of the whites lynched were lynched for helping the Black or being anti-lynching and even for domestic crimes." ("History of Lynchings").
18. Charles Lee Cook quoted in "Amity of races," *Evening Star*, 2.
19. Gregory, "Convention for Amity," 118.
20. Gregory, "Racial Amity," 654.

21. Louis Gregory quoted in Morrison, *To Move the World*, 134.
22. Representative Martin B. Hadden quoted in Gregory, "Convention for Amity," 118.
23. Mr. Alfred H. Martin quoted in Gregory, "Convention for Amity," 118.
24. Mills later worked closely with Shoghi Effendi on important legal matters related to Bahá'í communities including the Declaration of Trust and By-Laws of Bahá'í institutions (Authors' note).
25. Gregory, "Convention for Amity," 118.
26. Ibid., 115.
27. William H. Randall quoted in ibid., 119.
28. Warner, *Generals in Blue*, 323-324.
29. "Convention for Amity," 115.
30. Beginning in the 1920s, Mazandarani rendered an invaluable service by travelling throughout Iran to document the early history of the Bahá'í Faith, preserving the memory of events that had happened a little more than three generations earlier.
31. "Convention for Amity," 124.
32. Mazandarani quoted in ibid., 124.
33. Buck, "The Bahá'í 'Race Amity' Movement," 3.
34. 'Abdu'l-Bahá in letters to Agnes Parsons, 29 April 1921, 27 September 1921, and 29 April 1921, Bahá'í National Center, quoted in Morrison, *To Move the World*, 142. Historical document.
35. Gregory, "Racial Amity," 656-664.
36. 'Abdu'l-Bahá letter to Agnes Parsons, September 27, 1921, Bahá'í National Center, quoted in Morrison, *To Move the World*, 143. Historical document.
37. Shoghi Effendi, *God Passes By*, 310.
38. Ibid, 310.
39. 'Abdu'l-Bahá quoted in Shoghi Effendi and Lady Blomfield, "The Passing of 'Abdu'l-Bahá."
40. 'Abdu'l-Bahá quoted in Shoghi Effendi and Lady Blomfield, "The Passing of 'Abdu'l-Bahá."
41. Rabbani, *The Priceless Pearl*, 39.
42. Morrison, *To Move the World*, 151.
43. Ibid., 172.
44. Shoghi Effendi, *Bahá'í Administration*, 129, quoted in Morrison, *To Move the World*, 174.
45. Shoghi Effendi, ibid., 174.
46. Alfred Lunt to Louis Gregory, 4 August, 1927, quoted in Morrison, *To Move the World*, 179.
47. Louis Gregory in a letter to Agnes Parsons, 23 January, 1928, quoted in ibid., 177.

48. Shoghi Effendi in a letter to Louis Gregory, 31 October, 1928, quoted in ibid., 177.

Epilogue

Shoghi Effendi wrote a letter in 1938 to the American Bahá'ís, *The Advent of Divine Justice*, in which he sets forth the spiritual destiny of the nation and its role in achieving world peace. Bahá'ís must conduct themselves with moral rectitude and absolute chastity and become completely free of racial prejudice.

In addressing racial prejudice, Shoghi Effendi wrote:

> Freedom from racial prejudice, in any of its forms, should, at such a time as this when an increasingly large section of the human race is falling a victim to its devastating ferocity, be adopted as the watchword of the entire body of the American believers, in whichever state they reside, in whatever circles they move, whatever their age, traditions, tastes, and habits. It should be consistently demonstrated in every phase of their activity and life, whether in the Bahá'í community or outside it, in public or in private, formally as well as informally, individually as well as in their official capacity as organized groups, committees and Assemblies.[1]

He gave direct personal guidance to Black and white Bahá'ís:

> Let the white make a supreme effort in their resolve to contribute their share to the solution of this problem, to abandon once and for all their usually inherent and at times subconscious sense of superiority, to correct their tendency towards revealing a patronizing attitude towards the members of the other race, to persuade them through their intimate, spontaneous and

informal association with them of the genuineness of their friendship and the sincerity of their intentions, and to master their impatience of any lack of responsiveness on the part of a people who have received, for so long a period, such grievous and slow-healing wounds. Let the Negroes, through a corresponding effort on their part, show by every means in their power the warmth of their response, their readiness to forget the past, and their ability to wipe out every trace of suspicion that may still linger in their hearts and minds. Let neither think that the solution of so vast a problem is a matter that exclusively concerns the other. Let neither think that such a problem can either easily or immediately be resolved. Let neither think that they can wait confidently for the solution of this problem until the initiative has been taken, and the favorable circumstances created, by agencies that stand outside the orbit of their Faith. Let neither think that anything short of genuine love, extreme patience, true humility, consummate tact, sound initiative, mature wisdom, and deliberate, persistent, and prayerful effort, can succeed in blotting out the stain which this patent evil has left on the fair name of their common country. Let them rather believe, and be firmly convinced, that on their mutual understanding, their amity, and sustained cooperation, must depend, more than on any other force or organization operating outside the circle of their Faith, the deflection of that dangerous course so greatly feared by 'Abdu'lBahá, and the materialization of the hopes He cherished for their joint contribution to the fulfillment of that country's glorious destiny.[2]

Shoghi Effendi passed away in 1957. The Universal House of Justice, the eventual formation of which was called for in the Writings of Bahá'u'lláh, was first elected in 1963.

In a 2020, the Universal House of Justice urged the Bahá'ís to persevere in bringing the Bahá'í teachings into the visible world:

Sadly, however, your nation's history reveals that any significant progress toward racial equality has invariably been met by countervailing processes, overt or covert, that served to undermine the advances achieved and to reconstitute the forces of oppression by other means. Thus, whatever the immediate outcome of contemporary events, you need not be deterred, for you are cognizant of the 'long and thorny road, beset with pitfalls' described by the Guardian that still lies ahead. Your commitment to tread this road with determination and insight, drawing upon what you have learned in recent years about translating Bahá'u'lláh's teachings into reality, will have to be sustained until the time, anticipated by Shoghi Effendi, when you will have contributed your decisive share to the eradication of racial prejudice from the fabric of your nation.[3]

Notes

1.   Shoghi Effendi, *Advent of Divine Justice*, 36
2.   Ibid., 40.
3.   The Universal House of Justice, July 22, 2020.

Bibliography

Bahá'u'lláh
(1985 reprint). *The Hidden Words*. Wilmette IL: Bahá'í Publishing Trust.
(1988). *Tablets of Bahá'u'lláh Revealed After the Kitáb-i-Aqdas*. Wilmette IL: Bahá'í Publishing Trust.
(1988). *Epistle to the Son of the Wolf*. Wilmette IL: Bahá'í Publishing Trust.
(2005). *Gleanings from the Writings of Bahá'u'lláh*. Wilmette IL: Bahá'í Publishing Trust.

'Abdu'l-Bahá
(2010). *Some Answered Questions*. Wilmette, IL : US Bahá'í Publishing Trust.
(2006). *Paris Talks*. Wilmette, IL : US Bahá'í Publishing Trust.
(1982). *The Promulgation of Universal Peace*. Wilmette, IL : US Bahá'í Publishing Trust.
(1982). *Selections from the Writings of 'Abdu'l-Bahá*. Bahá'í World Centre.
(1909). *Tablets of Abdul-Baha Abbas*. 3 vols. New York: Baha'i Publishing Committee.
(1910). Tablet to Charles Mason Remey, *Star of the West*, v. 12, p.107. Chicago, IL: Bahá'í News Service.
(1921). Tablet to Mrs. Botay, *Star of the West*, v. 12, n. 3, p. 108. Chicago, IL: Bahá'í News Service.

Shoghi Effendi
(1990). *The Advent of Divine Justice*. Wilmette IL: Bahá'í Publishing Trust.
(1991). *The World Order of Baha'u'llah*. Wilmette IL: Bahá'í Publishing Trust.
(1988). *Lights of Guidance*. Bahá'í Publishing Trust.
(1922) with Lady Blomfield, "The Passing of 'Abdu'l-Baha," Haifa: Rosenfeld Bros. Accessed at https://bahai-library.com/shoghi-effendi_blomfield_passing_abdulbaha
(1974). *God Passes By*. Wilmette, IL: Baha'i Publishing Trust.

The Universal House of Justice
Message from the Universal House of Justice to the Bahá'ís of the United
States, 22 July, 2020, accessed at
https://www.bahai.org/library/authoritative-texts/
the-universal-house-of-justice/messages/20200722_001/1#870410255.

Ambar, Saladin. "Woodrow Wilson: Life Before the Presidency."
Accessed at https://millercenter.org/president/wilson/life-
before-the-presidency
Andrews, William D. (2008). "Dr. John George Gehring and His Bethel Clinic:
Pragmatic Therapy and Therapeutic Tourism." *Maine History* 43, 3 : 188-
216. https://digitalcommons.library.umaine.edu/mainehistoryjournal/
vol43/iss3/5
Asch, Chris Myers, and George Derek Musgrove. (2017). *Chocolate City:
A History of Race and Democracy in the Nation's Capital.* Chapel Hill:
University of North Carolina Press.
Auslander, Mark. "They Knew This Land." *Glover Park History.* Accessed
at https://gloverparkhistory.com/population/slaves-population/
mount-alban-highlands/
Randall-Winckler, Bahiyyih. (1996). *William Henry Randall.* London:
Oneworld.
Baghdadi, Dr. Zia. (1928-9). "'Abdu'l-Baha in America." *Star of the West,* Vol.
19, No. 7, 219.
Balyuzi, Hasan. (1972). *'Abdu'l-Baha, Centre of the Covenant.* Oxford, UK:
George Ronald.
_____. (1980). *Bahá'u'lláh: The King of Glory.* London: George Ronald.
Beamish, Richard Joseph and Francis Andrew March. (1919). *America's Part
in the World War: A History of the Full Greatness of Our Country's Achieve-
ments; the Record of the Mobilization and Triumph of the Military, Naval,
Industrial and Civilian Resources of the United States 1919.* Philadelphia:
The John C. Winston Company.
Blight, David W. (2001). *Race and Reunion: The Civil War in American
Memory.* Cambridge, MA: Harvard University Press.
Boyd, Herb. (2017). *Black Detroit: A People's History of Self-Determination.* New
York: Amistad, HarperCollins.
Buck, Christopher. "Despite Jim Crow, the Memphis Baha'is
Contemplate Integration." Accessed at https://bahaiteachings.org/
despite-jim-crow-the-memphis-bahais-contemplate-integration/.
_____. "The Baha'i 'Race Amity' Movement and the Black Intelligentsia in
Jim Crow America: Alain Locke and Robert S. Abbott," *Baha'i Studies
Review, Volume 17,* 3-46.

Buck, Christopher, with Steve Kolins. "African American Baha'is during Abdu'l-Baha's Time." Accessed at https://bahaiteachings.org/african-american-bahais-during-abdul-bahas-lifetime/.

Bryan, Jami L. "Fighting for respect: African-American Soldiers in WWI," accessed at https://armyhistory.org/fighting-for-respect-african-american-soldiers-in-wwi/.

Clewell, Beatriz Chu and Bernice Taylor Anderson. (1995). "African Americans in Higher Education: An Issue of Access." *Humboldt Journal of Social Relations*, vol. 21, n. 2, African-Americans in the 1990s, 55-79. Department of Sociology: Humboldt State University.

Davis, Gordon J. (2015). "Wilson, Princeton, and Race." *The New York Times*, November 24. Accessed at http://www.nytimes.com/2015/11/24/opinion/what-woodrow-wilson-cost-my-grandfather.html.

DeFerrari, John. "How Sweet It Was: Washington's Great Caterer-Confectioners," *Streets of Washington*. Accessed at http://www.streetsofwashington.com/2014/06/how-sweet-it-was-washingtons-great.

Dodge, Wendell Phillips. (1912). "Abdu'l-Baha's Arrival in America." *Star of the West*, Volume 3, pp. 3-6. Chicago: Baha'i News Service.

DuBois, W. E. B. (2007). *Dusk of Dawn*. Oxford, UK: Oxford University Press.

_____. "The College-bred Negro American." Edited by W. E. Burghardt Du Bois and Augustus Granville Dill. Atlanta University Press, Atlanta, GA. 1910. Page 12. Accessed at http://scua.library.umass.edu/digital/dubois/dubois15.pdf on October 19 2020.

Eliot, Samuel Atkins. (1914). "Harvey Stuart Chase." *Biographical History of Massachusetts, vol. 5*. Massachusetts Biographical Society.

Etter-Lewis, Gwendolyn, Richard Thomas, and Richard Walter (2006). *Lights of the Spirit: Historical Portraits of Black Bahá'ís in North America, 1898-2004*. Wilmette, IL: Bahá'í Publishing Trust.

Francis, Richard. (1998). "Amoz Everett Gibson: The First Black Member of the Universal House of Justice." Accessed at https://bahai-library.com/francis_gibson_biography

Gail, Marzieh. (1991). *Arches of the Years*. Oxford, UK: George Ronald.

Gregory, Louis. letter to a friend in Tulsa, OK, Nov. 25, 1916, *Star of the West*, v. 7, n. 16. Chicago, IL: Baha'i News Service. 158.

_____. (1936). "Racial Amity in America: A Historical Overview," *Bahá'í World*, 1932-1934, v. 5, 655-670. New York: Bahá'í Publishing Committee.

_____. (1921). "Convention for Amity Between the Colored and White Races." *Star of the West*, v. 12, n. 6. Chicago: Baha'i News Service. 115-119, 123-124.

_____. (1911). *A Heavenly Vista: The Pilgrimage of Louis G. Gregory*. R. L. Pendleton, Washington, D.C. 1911. Bahá'í Library Online, https://bahai-library.com/gregory_heavenly_vista.

_____. *"Some Recollections of the Early Days of the Bahai Faith in Washington,*

D.C.," MS, *Louis G. Gregory* Papers, National Bahá'í Archives of the United States, Wilmette, Illinois.

Gustkey, Earl. (8 July 1990). "80 Years Ago, the Truth Hurt : Johnson's Victory Over Jeffries Taught Lesson to White America". *Los Angeles Times.*

Hannen, Joseph. (1912). "Abdul-Baha in Washington DC." *Star of the West*, v. 3, n. 3, p. 6. Chicago: Bahá'í News Service.

_____. (1910)."Washington DC", *Baha'i News*, v. 1, n. 1, March 21. Chicago: Baha'i News Service, 18-19.

_____. (1910), "Washington DC", *Baha'i News*, v. 1, n. 3, April 28. Chicago: Baha'i News Service, 18-19.

_____. (1910), "Washington DC", *Baha'i News*, v. 1, n. 2, April 9. Chicago: Baha'i News Service, 13.

Hearst, Phoebe. "Two letters from Phoebe Hearst." *Bahá'í World, 1936-1938*, *v. 7*, 800-801. New York: Bahá'í Publishing Committee.

Hemphill, James C. (1917). "Franklin Knight Lane." *The North American Review, Vol. 206, No. 741.* University of Northern Iowa.

Higgins, Abigail. "Red Summer of 1919: How Black WWI Vets Fought Back Against Racist Mobs." Accessed at https://www.history.com/news/red-summer-1919-riots-chicago-dc-great-migration.

Hine, Darlene Clark. (2005). *Black Women in America: A-G.* Oxford, UK: Oxford University Press.

Holub, Florence. "Florence's Family Album: From the Ashes of 1906." Accessed at http://www.noevalleyvoice.com/2001/April/Flor.html.

Katz, William Loren. (1967). *Eyewitness: The Negro in American History.* New York: Pitman Publishing Corporation.

Khademi, Mona. "Glimpses into the Life of Laura Dreyfus-Barney." *Lights of Irfan, v. 10.* Wilmette, IL: Irfan Colloquia. 71-106.

_____. Unpublished bio of Laura Dreyfus Barney.

Kraft, Barbara Sarina. (1976). *Some Must Dream: The History of the Ford Peace Expedition and the Neutral Conference for Continuous Mediation.* Ph.D. thesis in Philosophy of History, the American University.

Lowery, Rev. L. E. "Rev. L.E. Lowery's Column." *The Southern Indicator*, February 19, 1921. Accesed at https://www.newspapers.com/clip/3099456/soon-bahai-louis-g-gregory-with/.

Lunardini, Christine A. (1979). "William Monroe Trotter's Meetings with Woodrow Wilson, 1913-1914." *The Journal of Negro History*, Vol. 64, No. 3 (Summer, 1979). pp. 244-264. Chicago: The University of Chicago Press on behalf of the Association for the Study of AfricanAmerican Life and History.

Maxwell, May. (1917). *An Early Pilgrimage.* Oxford, UK: George Ronald. https://bahai-library.com/maxwell_early_pilgrimage

Mayo, Lynette. "The Greater Orlando Baha'i Center." Harvard University Pluralism Project's Rollins College Affiliate program. Accessed at https://sites.fas.harvard.edu/~pluralsm/affiliates/greenberg/bahai.history.html.

McHenry, Elizabeth. (2002). *Recovering the Lost History of African American Literary Societies*. Durham, NC: Duke University Press.

McKay, Doris. (1973). "Devoted Handmaiden, Mrs. Agnes Parsons." *Baha'i News*, July, 1973. Wilmette, IL: National Spiritual Assembly of the Bahá'ís of the United States.

Meier, August and Elliott Rudwick. (1967). "The Rise of Segregation in the Federal Bureaucracy, 1900-1930," *Phylon*. Vol 28, No. 2 (2nd Qtr, 1967).

Moe, Judy Hannen. (2019). *Aflame with Devotion: The Hannen and Knobloch Families and the Early Days of the Bahá'í Faith in America*. Wilmette IL: Bahá'í Publishing Trust.

Morrison, Gayle. (1995). *To Move the World: Louis Gregory and the Advancement of Racial Unity in America*. Wilmette IL: Bahá'í Publishing Trust.

_____. "Gregory, Louis George." *The Bahá'í Encyclopedia Project*. Accessed at https://www.bahai-encyclopedia-project.org

Ober, Harlan F. "Louis G. Gregory." *Bahá'í World, 1950-1954*, v. 12, 666-670. Wilmette IL: Bahá'í Publishing Trust.

Parsons, Agnes. Edited by Richard Hollinger. (1996). *The Diary of Agnes Parsons*. Los Angeles: Kalimat Press.

Rabbaní, Ruhiyyih. (1969).*The Priceless Pearl*. London: Bahá'í Publishing Trust.

Richard Rothstein. "On renaming the Woodrow Wilson School," April 14, 2016. Accessed at https://www.epi.org/blog/on-renaming-the-woodrow-wilson-school-the-standards-of-his-time-and-ours/.

Ruhe-Schoen, Janet. (2015). *Champions of Oneness*. Wilmette, IL: Bahá'í Publishing Trust.

Sauer, Patrick. "One Hundred Years Ago, a Four-Day Race Riot Engulfed Washington D.C."   Accessed at https://www.smithsonianmag.com/history/one-hundred-years-ago-four-day-race-riot-engulfed-washington-dc-180972666/.

Sennett, Frank. "Hall of Hate", www.weeklywire.com retrieved October 19, 2020. http://weeklywire.com/ww/08-03-98/chicago_cover2.html

Snowden-McCray, Lisa. (2019). "The NAACP Was Established February 12, 1909." *The Crisis*. Retrieved July 28, 2020.

Mirza Ahmad Sohrab. (1929). *Abdu'l-Baha in Egypt*. New York: New History Foundation.

Stockman, Robert. (1995). *The Bahá'í Faith in America: Origins, v. 1 and v.2, 1892-1900*. Wilmette IL: Bahá'í Publishing Trust.

_____. (1995). "Knobloch, Fanny." https://bahai-library.com/stockman_knobloch

_____. "Remey, Charles Mason." https://bahai-library.com/stockman_remey.

Statistical Abstract Supplement No. HS-2. Population Characteristics: 1900 to 2002, of the United States: 2003, Census. U.S. Census Bureau, 2003. Accessed at https://www2.census.gov/library/publications/2004/compendia/statab/123ed/hist/hs-02.pdf on October 19 2020.

Stein, Edward. (2004). "Past and Present Proposed Amendments to the United States Constitution." *Washington University Law Quarterly*, v. 82. n. 3, 612-666.

Taft, William Howard. "Inaugural Address of William Howard Taft." Accessed at https://avalon.law.yale.edu/20th_century/taft.asp.

Terborg-Penn, Rosalyn. (1998). *African American Women in the Struggle for the Vote: 1850-1920.* Bloomington, IN: Indiana University Press.

The Sage of the Potomac, "Public Men and Things." *The Washington Bee.* 07 Jan 1911, Saturday, 1. Washington DC: Bee Publishing Company.

University of Kentucky Libraries. "Notable Kentucky African Americans – Marshall, Harriet (Hattie) A. Gibbs." nkaa.uky.edu.

Ward, Allan L. (1979). *239 Days: Abdu'l-Bahá's Journey in America.* Wilmette Il: Baha'i Publishing Trust.

Warner, Ezra J. (1964). *Generals in Blue: Lives of the Union Commanders.* Baton Rouge, LA: Louisiana State University Press.

Weiss, Nancy J. (1969). "The Negro and the New Freedom: Fighting Wilsonian Segregation." *Political Science Quarterly* 84.

Wray, L. Randall. (2004). *Credit and state theories of money: the contributions of A. Mitchell Innes.* Cheltenham, UK: Edward Elgar Pub.

Whitehead, O.Z. (1976). *Some Early Bahá'ís of the West.* Oxford, UK: George Ronald.

Zarandi, Nabil. Translated by Shoghi Effendi. (1932). *The Dawnbreakers.* Wilmette IL: Bahá'í Publishing Trust.

Zarqani, Mahmud-i. *Mahmud's Diary.* Oxford, UK: George Ronald.

No Author Given

"'Abdu'l-Bahá talks of Universal Peace." *Washington (DC) Herald.* November 7, 1912, Washington, DC.

"Ali Kuli Khan." https://bahaipedia.org/Ali_Kuli_Khan#Service_in_America.

"Amity of races urged by speakers." *Evening Star.* Washington DC, 20 May 1921.

"Benevolent Society Incorporated." *Evening Star.* Washington, DC. Jan. 12 1900, p. 14.

"Catharine E. Nourse 1904—1985." *Bahá'í World, 1950-1954, v. 12,* 681-684. Wilmette IL: Bahá'í Publishing Trust. 680-681.

"Coralie Franklin Cook." *Democrat and Chronicle.* 28 November, 1902, Friday, 11.

"The Delta Sigma Theta Sorority." *The Mirror*. Howard University Yearbooks. Book 94.

"Ella Goodall Cooper." *Bahá'í World, 1950-1954, v. 12*, 681-684. Wilmette IL: Bahá'í Publishing Trust.

"Edward Bruce Moore." "https://www.uspto.gov/about-us/edward-bruce-moore.

"Fire and Ice: Adolphus W. Greely." https://www.armyheritage.org/soldier-stories/fire-ice-adolphus-w-greely.

"The First Nine Days." *Baha'i News*, n. 516, March, 1974, 9-19.

"Fisher, Walter Lowrie (1862-1935)." accessed at https://digital.janeaddams.ramapo.edu/items/show/425.

"Francis David Millet and Millet Family Papers, 1858-1984." *Smithsonian Institution, Virtual Archives*, https://sova.si.edu/record/AAA.millfran?s=30&n=10&t=C&q=Drummers+%28Musicians%29&i=35.

"Ghodsia Ashraf Khanum." *Star of the West*, v. 2, n. 7-8, p. 7-8. Chicago, IL: Bahá'í News Service.

"Henry Billings Brown, United States Jurist." Accessed at https://www.britannica.com/biography/Henry-Billings-Brown.

"Henry H. Jessup makes an Eloquent and Instructive Address." *The Inter Ocean*. Chicago, Illinois. 24 September, 1893, 2.

"History." https://www.sixthandi.org/about/history/.

"History of Lynchings." https://www.naacp.org/history-of-lynchings/.

"History and Legacy." https://chapel.howard.edu/about/history-and-legacy.

"Leila Young Payne." https://bahaipedia.org/Leila_Young_Payne.

"A Legacy of Vision." https://www.whctemple.org/about/history/senior-rabbis/.

"NAACP : Charles Hamilton Houston." Accessed at https://www.naacp.org/naacp-history-charles-hamilton-houston.

"No Negro Wanted." *Washington Bee*, Saturday, March 9, 1907. Accessed at https://www.newspapers.com/clip/3099456/soon-bahai-louis-g-gregory-with/.

"Notable Descendants." *General Society of Mayflower Descendants*. Accessed at https://www.themayflowersociety.org/the-pilgrims/notable-descendants.

"World's Parliament of Religions." Accessed at https://www.encyclopedia.com/religion/encyclopedias-almanacs-transcripts-and- maps/worlds-parliament-religion.

"Paul Edmond Haney." (1986). *The Bahá'í World*, vol. XVIII. Bahá'í World Centre: Haifa.

"Persian-American Educational Society." *Star of the West*, v. 1, n. 1, p. 13. Chicago, IL: Bahá'í News Service.

"The Persian-American Educational Society." *Star of the West*, v. 1, n. 5, p. 4-6. Chicago, IL: Bahá'í News Service.

"Mrs. Phoebe Hearst dies in California." *New York Times,* April 14, 1919, 13.

"Pocahontas Kay Grizzard Pope." Accessed at https://bahaipedia.org/Pocahontas_Kay_Grizzard_Pope#cite_ref-Orsotemail_18-0.

"Rockwood Hoar Papers." Accessed at https://www.masshist.org/collection-guides/view/fa0138.

"Wainwright to Leave the Navy." *The Princeton Union*, Thursday, December 21, 1911.

"Washington's Most Curious Cult—Under Leadership of a Woman." Washington Post, October 31, 1909.

"Washington Conservatory of Music." *The Colored American*. October 24, 1903, 11.

"The Week in Society." *The Washington Bee*, 06 Nov., 1909, 5.

"William Bedford Royall." 2011. http://www.arlingtoncemetery.net/wbroyall.htm.

Made in the USA
Middletown, DE
28 August 2024

59937366R00124